The Holy Eucharist: Rite Two

The Holy Eucharist: Rite Two
A Devotional Commentary

DONALD J. PARSONS

A CROSSROAD BOOK
THE SEABURY PRESS · NEW YORK

The Seabury Press
815 Second Avenue
New York, N.Y. 10017

Printed in the United States of America

Library of Congress Cataloging in Publication Data

Parsons, Donald J   1922–
   The Holy Eucharist, rite two.

   "A Crossroad book."
   1. Protestant Episcopal Church in the U.S.A
Liturgical Commission. The draft proposed of Common
Prayer. The Holy Eucharist, rite two. 2. Lord's
Supper (Liturgy) I. Title.
BX5944.C75P37   264'.035   76–15636
ISBN 0–8164–2129–3

To the people and clergy of
the Diocese of Quincy

Contents

The Holy Eucharist: Rite Two

Introduction

The Second Service for the Eucharist begins so differently from the 1928 Prayer Book rite. Some people are jubilant, some are resentful, and some have mixed feelings about the difference. The purpose of this book is to encourage a more prayerful and thoughtful use of the Second Service by those who welcome the change and those who find they can live with it without either enthusiasm or repugnance. Yet a special concern is shown for those who are hurt, confused, and angered by the alteration of the Prayer Book rite they know so well and love so deeply. Verbal missiles of many types have been hurled at these unhappy Episcopalians, and many of the charges leveled against them have been unfair as well as uncharitable. Do we really know enough about the inner workings of our fellows to accuse them of an idolatry of Elizabethan language or of similar sins? In liturgical disputes there seems to be a temptation to forget that we have been told, "So pass no premature judgement; wait until the Lord comes. For he will bring to light what darkness hides, and disclose men's inward motives; then will be the time for each to receive from God such praise as he deserves" (I Cor. 4:5).

This author believes that there are many reasons why people cling to the 1928 Prayer Book service. One reason is that certain words or phrases have, over the years, come to possess deep personal significance for human beings. Perhaps it was at the death of a favorite aunt that somehow a particular phrase in the Prayer Book came alive, spoke to the individual in a powerful way, and so became a part of the inner buttressing of the person's whole approach to life. Perhaps at the birth of one's first child or at one's first significant promotion, something like that occurred. Or perhaps it was one day when someone was terribly lonely or especially discouraged that some words of the Communion Service became not just words on a page but a part of his or her life. Here may be the real reason why some persons react so strongly to changes other people think are justified by liturgical research and theological excellence. The author believes that many persons are in exactly this position and that verbal abuse is neither justified nor helpful. We may, however, offer some help if we can show that the new liturgy also has phrases which speak to our condition, that it is possible to pray the Second Service too and not just suffer under it. The intention behind this book is neither debate about liturgical superiority nor a not-so-subtle selling job, but a desire to see how both the enthusiastic and the reluctant can better pray the Second Service.

1. Blessed Be God

Blessed be God: Father, Son, and Holy Spirit.
And blessed be his kingdom, now and for ever. Amen.

Blessed be God

In the very beginning the new service is quite different. No longer do we enter upon the Eucharist in a quiet, subdued, and even somewhat penitential mood. Instead we begin with an acclamation, an outburst of praise and thanksgiving to God. "Blessed be God" is the characteristic form of prayer in the Old Testament and in Jewish worship, both corporate and individual. It reminds us, as it does the Jews, that God is not someone we seek but someone who came seeking us. For the Jew, God called to Moses from the midst of the burning bush, brought Israel out of bondage, and then revealed himself on Sinai. God acted first, and the Jew responds in awe and thanksgiving to the goodness by which he was surprised and which he had not even thought to seek. For the Christian the story is re-emphasized. The eternal Son became man, not when we decided to ask for it but at the time the Father willed. The tomb was left behind by the risen Christ not because the disciples hoped for it nor because they expected it. Instead Christ rose and appeared to his chosen witnesses to their great surprise, producing first trembling and astonishment, then gradual recognition, and finally joy.

In the Communion Service we come to worship, and sometimes it takes a lot of effort to get ourselves there. Unconsciously we can therefore become absorbed by our efforts to seek Christ, by our attempts to serve him, and our endeavors to worship him. It is salutary to be bluntly reminded in the very beginning that we are really here in church because God sought us and not the other way around. We exist because he created us; we come to the Eucharist because Christ instituted it and promised to be present when in obedience we break the bread, and because the Holy Spirit draws us to worship and will do the praying in us. We are challenged to begin by looking at God, not at ourselves. It is right to begin in this thankful fashion, because our lives come from the Father, our hope of rescue is in the Son, and our longing for a better self is the work of the Spirit within.

Yet what can we do if we do not feel this way when we come to church? What if our mood is not one of thanksgiving and joy and confident faith? Is it deceptive or unreal for us to begin with these words of praise if our feelings are so very different? Not at all, because truth exists no matter what our emotions may be. It is good that God is what he is, even though at the moment our mood is at odds with that truth. It is false to pretend joyfulness when we do not have it, but it is not false to proclaim a truth we accepted with both mind and will, even if at this moment our emotions refuse to coincide. There are many reasons why it is not false to act thus, but two of these reasons might be looked at more fully.

First, the faith being proclaimed in the service is the

faith of the Church, of the whole Body of Christ. We worship not as isolated individuals but as members of Christ's Church. What we as individuals might be able to say in only a tentative and timid fashion the Church can trumpet with assurance, and it is not false for us to share in that acclamation. No one human being could presume to think he can adequately comprehend the action of the infinite God. Indeed all of us together cannot do it either, but certainly the Church as a whole is a little better equipped for this understanding. St. Paul writes, "May you be strong to grasp, with all God's people, what is the breadth and length and height and depth of the love of Christ, and to know it, though it is beyond knowledge" (Eph. 3:18–19). "With all God's people" we may grasp more than we can alone, even though together we still find that divine truth "is beyond knowledge." One of the values of common worship is that our own individual faith is strengthened, deepened, and even probed by the faith of the community. More than one person has found this true, for example, while participating in the Burial Office. Unhappy and perplexed, he comes to a funeral and finds that the sturdy faith of the Church, proclaimed in that service, strengthens and expands his own. The same thing happens in the other services of the Church, and there is nothing fake about joining our little bit of faith to the vigor and fullness of the Church's confession. The uncertain and trembling recruit has a right to march in his regiment's ranks; time and testing will someday make him a dependable veteran too.

Second, we can honestly join in this acclamation of praise because we neither intend to deceive the Lord nor are we able to do so. If we do not feel confident and ready to praise him, he knows it, and we know he does. For this reason we may be grateful that the much-loved Collect for Purity follows right away. To God our hearts are open, and from him no secrets are hidden. We acknowledge it, and we are grateful that we do not have to pretend before him. We can honestly say "Blessed be God," because we know it is right and true to say it even though some present clouds of life keep our emotions from fitting the words. Indeed that treasured prayer reminds us that only by the inspiration of his Holy Spirit can we hope to worthily magnify God's holy Name. There is no pretense in praising him. Whether we feel it or not, it is still true to begin by crying, "Blessed be God."

And blessed be his kingdom

We thank God for being, and we praise him for being what he is. Yet he not only exists; he also acts, and we rejoice at his acting. This truth is the one expressed by the acclamation "Blessed be his kingdom." Yet the word "kingdom" may obscure the cause for the rejoicing. "Kingdom" suggests a place, a certain portion of territory. One is therefore in a kingdom or not in it; a kingdom is either here or not here. So we tend to think of God's kingdom as a future thing, or if we think of it as present we may draw a picture of it that is unreal or falsely narrow. Hence the New Testament scholars may be helpful and not just pedantic when they suggest that a better translation is the word "kingship." Someone's kingship is true even if there are rebels in his territory who deny it, even though it is still in the process of being actualized, or even if those who acknowledge his kingship are as yet inconsistent in their obedience. God is king of the earth, even though evil resists his reigning or even denies his existence. He is king over the world and over the Church.

But within the Church his kingship is acknowledged and proclaimed.

We give thanks that God's kingship is becoming more evident in history and in our personal histories. His kingship is actualized in the obedient life of Jesus, in the casting out of evil by Jesus' deeds of mercy and of healing, and by the raising of Jesus out of the grip of death. It is actualized in human history as over the centuries there has been a painfully slow, often spasmodic, but still evident advance of goodness. We may fail to perceive much advance, but the human race once saw nothing wrong with exposing unwanted infants on hillsides or throwing them into the Tiber, once thought slavery was inevitable and even right, once thought the insane were demons to be chained, and once thought women were pieces of property and less than fully human. The advances have not been steady, nor are they irreversible. Yet we can and should give thanks that God's kingship is more evident now than it was once.

Likewise the kingship of God is somewhat more fully recognized in our own lives than once was true. We cannot brag about it, because goodness is his doing and not our own. We dare not exaggerate it nor imagine that the task is anywhere near completion, but neither is it true to deny what change there has been. Perhaps our lives are not very different, perhaps the longing has not yet produced much fruit, and assuredly our little growth has brought an awareness that our sinfulness is deeper and more subtle than we once realized. Yet the fact that we long for something better is a sign of the Spirit's work, and perceiving the depth of our need is at least one more step toward the light. We are rather unsteady and undependable subjects, but at least we have been enabled to confess God as our lord and king. Honesty demands that we admit the feebleness of our growth, but the very same honesty must acknowledge any growth that has taken place. We may still be impatient, but we may also be struggling more against the impatience. We may still be needlessly critical, but perhaps there have been at least a few times we have kept silent or a few persons we have come to understand a little more truly. The Gospel does not only tell us how we ought to live, it also promises a power for new living. Surely there has been some advance, even in us, and it is right to thank God for it. He does not merely possess kingship, he exercises it. For every trace of this kingship, for every inch of its advancement, "Blessed be his kingdom, now and for ever. Amen."

2. Let Us Confess

Let us confess our sins against God and our neighbor.
Most merciful God,
we confess that we have sinned against you
in thought, word, and deed,
by what we have done,
and by what we have left undone.
We have not loved you with our whole heart;
we have not loved our neighbors as ourselves.
We are truly sorry and we humbly repent.
For the sake of your Son Jesus Christ,
have mercy on us and forgive us;
that we may delight in your will,
and walk in your ways,
to the glory of your Name. Amen.
Almighty God have mercy on you, forgive you all your sins
through our Lord Jesus Christ, strengthen you in all goodness,
and by the power of the Holy Spirit keep you in eternal life.

The presence in the new liturgy of a fairly full form of confession is at once evidence of "the power of the people" and the willingness of the revisers to listen to what the people said. When the revision process began, there was a widespread consensus that the old rite still suffered from that excessively penitential note characteristic of all the sixteenth-century revisions. There was a strong desire to achieve a truer balance of penitence and thanksgiving, of crucifixion and resurrection, of sacrifice and victory. The pendulum could easily have swung too far the other way, but the "man in the pew" helped preserve a more balanced approach. This fact of history should demonstrate that the penitential element in the service is not the work of morbid clergy nor the mere preservation of traditional material to placate the liturgical scholar. The people's reaction was probably more of an instinctive affair than an intellectual one, but instinct can sometimes be a surer guide to the truth. Reason, however, still has the task of trying to discover why that instinct was so right. So we need to ask why confession is necessary and what there is for us to confess.

Why should we confess our sins before we worship God? Surely not because he demands a bit of groveling on our part before he will visit us. God spoke to Moses before those poor captives in Egypt had begun to hope he would save them, and Christ died for us "while we were yet sinners." Furthermore, we cheapen the fact of God's forgiveness if we think of it as something we get from him by successful whining and wheedling. We need to ask for forgiveness because we cannot receive it until we know we require it. God ceaselessly extends mercy, but he cannot make us take something we do not admit to ourselves that we need. What psychiatrists teach about guilt reactions can help us understand why we must confess our sins. When we injure someone else, we are uncomfortable in that person's presence; we seek to hide from the injured one or find some way of assuring ourselves that it is really the other person's fault anyway. Our discomfort makes us either avoid or be angry with the one we have injured. We cannot worship God or come into his presence, if we are seeking to hide from him or are secretly angry toward him. We need to uncover our guilt and admit it is our own fault. We cannot *make* God come to us but we must be able to *let* him come near to us.

But what are these sins of which we are guilty? Perhaps we are not aware that we have sinned, and we do not see ourselves as truly affected by guilt feelings. More than one confessor has heard a penitent say, "I don't think I've sinned since my last confession." Usually this means "Since then I have neither robbed a bank, committed adultery, nor murdered anyone." So let us look at some words in the Confession: "we have sinned against you in thought, word, and deed, by what we have done, and by what we have left undone." Perhaps we can truly claim we have not *done* anything wrong. What about those thoughts, however? How many little dramas have we worked out in our imagination, little scenarios in which we really got even with that supervisor, found the truly devastating words to cut that big shot down to size, or watched that envied rival fall flat on his face? But what is so wrong about that? Dreams of revenge, of triumph over others, of getting even—these smoldering embers have a way of breaking forth in flames someday. How else explain the fact that we have on occasion discovered ourselves saying bitter words we never intended to say or doing things we never thought we would do?

We have sinned also "by what we have done, and by what we have left undone." If we can truly claim to have avoided the first category, it is most unlikely that we have escaped the second. The "left undone" clause covers so much: the letter to a lonely old relative that was not written, the word of thanks we forgot to speak, the injustice we saw but preferred to ignore or the injustice we never noticed because of our self-absorption, the helping hand we did not extend, the awkward outsider we brushed past, or the tale of sorrow we had no time to hear. In a world filled with so many lonely persons, with so many desperately unhappy souls, with so many anxious human beings, the "left undone" may be the greatest sin of all. How deep the tragedy if "I didn't do anything wrong" really means "I didn't do anything." Our time on this earth is too short to have the epitaph read, "We have not loved."

Have mercy on us and forgive us;
that we may delight in your will,
and walk in your ways.

We ask God to "have mercy on us and forgive us" not only in order that we may be able to rejoice in his presence but in order that we may serve him better. We need then to notice the words "walk" and "in your ways." Both phrases are solidly biblical ones. Christianity is described not as a collection of dogmas but as a "way" (Acts 9:2), and the description of godly living in terms of walking has an extensive Old Testament background as well as a New Testament one. A single reference should suffice: "At the same time he is the father of such of the circumcised as do not rely upon their circumcision alone, but also walk in the footprints of the faith which our father Abraham had while he was yet uncircumcised" (Rom. 4:12). Behind those two words lies the sturdy and unsentimental emphasis of the Bible that religion involves more than feelings, ecstatic experiences, and exalted ideas. As the greatest teacher put it:

Beware of false prophets, men who come to you dressed up as a sheep while underneath they are savage wolves. You will recognize them by the fruits they bear. Can grapes be picked from briars, or figs from thistles? In the same way, a good tree always yields good fruit, and a poor tree bad fruit. (Mt. 7: 15–17)

The Lord desires, however, not only that we may obey but that we shall find joy in doing so. His commands are not arbitrary things designed to bring him pleasure; they seek to keep us safe from the things which destroy or embitter human lives, both our own and those of others. So God would have us "delight" in his will, not just observe it in a grumpy and reluctant fashion. It is indeed a delight to have some assurance of what is right, some warning of what is in fact destructive, some insight into what is truly good and honorable and worthwhile. To speak of obedience and of delight in the same breath at first seems not only peculiar but almost ridiculous. How much anxious strain, however, have we felt when we wished to do the right thing but were not so sure what it was in some particular situation? We have been bitterly remorseful also upon discovering that some well-intentioned project brought not only failure but also did a good deal of harm. We have been shamed when we at last came to perceive that we spoiled something precious by neglect or impatience or inappropriate hidden motives. To delight in God's will is not an absurdity when we are dealing with the Lord who in his teaching and in his life unites obedience and love and joy. "If you heed my commands, you will dwell in my love, as I have heeded my Father's commands and dwell in his love. I have spoken thus to you, so that my joy may be in you, and your joy complete" (Jn. 15:10–11).

**Almighty God . . . keep you
in eternal life.**

We tend to think of eternal life as something toward
which we move, something for which we hope in the
future. It is hard to grasp the theological truth that for the
believer eternal life has already begun and that the believer needs to keep within this life rather than be
brought to it. Baptism, however, does mark our being led
into eternal life as we are made, by God's action, members
of the Body of Christ and inheritors of God's kingdom.
Eternal life, that is, a certain quality and not just length
of life, is already given, and we by faith already share in
it. Although we have learned this truth intellectually, we
may still find it less than real for us personally. We still
seem so far away from God, still so unsteady in our walking and so inconstant in our striving. Are there not, however, other facts we know by experience? There have
been some occasional examples of fidelity and some frag-
ments of goodness. Were they our doing? We know that
goodness is in God and comes from him. If there has been
anything worthwhile in us, it is evidence that he does
indeed live in us and we live in him. We may be surprised
by the evil we do and take the good for granted, whereas
the really surprising fact is the presence of goodness in
such creatures as ourselves. Then too, there have been
some moments when prayer was real, when in worship
we knew Someone else was there, when there came some
touch of longing or of joy that transcended ordinary explanation. We do not claim any visions such as those given to
some of the saints, but neither should we downgrade what
has been granted us. Like Paul we feel, "faith is our guide,
we do not see him" (II Cor. 5:7), but there have been those
touches of assurance that he is not only a God far off but
also near.

Merely being kept in eternal life may not appear to be very exciting. It may seem static while we desire something more stirring and active. We do know, however, that there are times when hanging on firmly is all we can do, times when the winds are fierce and the waves high. We may not seem to be going ahead, but there are periods when standing fast is quite an achievement. Scripture is realistic about this fact, as about so many other facets of human experience. St. Paul was as enthusiastic as any of us, and his personality made him as eager as any of us to go forward, to advance, to climb higher. Even he, however, has a lot to say about standing fast. Indeed he expresses it in stirring words: "Therefore, take up God's armour; then you will be able to stand your ground when things are at their worst, to complete every task and still to stand" (Eph. 6:13).

We need to "stand our ground" many times in the course of our earthly pilgrimage. Experience, however, may make us unsure that we will always do it. It matters to know then that God is in us and with us at those tough times too. We cannot be so sure of ourselves, but we can be sure of him. Jesus knew what his disciples were like, just as he knows our weaknesses and appalling instability. Yet he also knew the Father's power and his unchanging purpose. Hence he said, "I give them eternal life and they shall never perish; no one shall snatch them from my care. My Father who has given them to me is greater than all, and no one can snatch them out of the Father's care" (Jn. 10: 28–29).

3. The Peace of the Lord

The peace of the Lord be always with you.

There is a special irony in the fact that the Peace is that part of the new liturgy which has provoked the most controversy and the greatest unhappiness. The fact is so incongruous, so obviously inappropriate, that we must take special pains to understand what this liturgical practice is all about. It is hard to evaluate something through a fog of emotion, and therefore the first step is to distinguish as clearly as possible between the Peace itself and the manner in which it is performed. For some it is offensive to have a solemn service suddenly interrupted by a boisterous exchange of embraces, by loud greetings and unrestrained backslapping. It seems so out of place and so unfitting that some parishioners would do away with the Peace entirely. Yet there is a difference between the thing itself and the manner in which it is executed. Perhaps we can be helped to make this needed distinction by taking time to look at some elements that affect the way in which the Peace is exchanged.

The liturgy is celebrated in and by a gathering of Christians, and the character of that gathering affects the way the celebration is done. For example, the type of music used in a great cathedral parish would not fit in a little country mission, as experience has repeatedly shown. Just so, the manner of exchanging the Peace depends in part upon the nature of the community that is doing it. One style may be fitting for a small group of Christians who have come to know each other well and to share deeply, as with a Cursillo group at the end of their weekend together. The same may be true of a seminary community whose members have been living together, praying together, studying together, and working together day after day in a common setting. Would the same kind of interchange be appropriate in a large parish whose membership is heterogeneous, whose sense of community is much more tenuous, and whose coming together is much less frequent and less intense? True, we want a real sense of community in a parish, but realistically such a spirit often is not that powerful and to some extent cannot be. It may be artificial or even phony to extend the Peace in a parish setting in a way that would be entirely right in a smaller group setting.

Furthermore, the gathered community is made up of different persons, with differing temperaments, life styles, and cultural patterns. Some are by nature outgoing and even exuberant creatures, while others are shy, reserved, and more cautious in personal contacts. If we really mean "The peace of the Lord be always with you," we need to take the "you" seriously. That other person is the way he or she is, and accepting the other person includes an acceptance of his or her nature. Love for neighbor should include some sensitivity to the neighbor's feelings. It certainly should exclude any tendency to judge the shy person as "cold" or the outgoing one as "aggressive" or "imposing." Love will help us meet and respect our neighbor as he or she is.

Having tried to distinguish between the manner of act-

ing and the thing itself, we must go on and seek to discover why the Peace has been included in the revised
liturgy. The revisers will certainly reply that the exchange
of the kiss of peace is found in the very earliest forms of
the Eucharist and their claim is wholly justified. We find
the practice alluded to in the *Apostolic Tradition* of Hippolytus of Rome, a third-century document. It is mentioned even earlier in the writings of Justin Martyr (about
155 AD). Even more important, the holy kiss is mentioned
often in the brief commands found at the end of several
Pauline epistles (Rom. 16:16, I Th. 5:26, II Cor. 13:12).
Among New Testament scholars there is widespread acceptance of the belief that these references show the kiss
of peace to have been a part of the Eucharist as celebrated
by those primitive Christian congregations.[1] Paul's letters
were to be read to the whole congregation, and the one
time the whole group would be gathered would be at the
Eucharist on the Lord's Day. So those brief little sent-
ences at the end of several epistles reflect the worship of
our earliest Christian brothers and sisters. As we exchange
the Peace, we act as did those early believers in the little
congregations that listened to the sermons of St. Paul.

Is this fact anything more than mere antiquarianism?
Shall we revive a practice just because the early Christians did it, or do we not have to ask why they did it?
There appear to be two elements in their thinking. One
was the aspect of reconciliation with one's neighbor before coming to worship God, an injunction which we have
seen goes back to Jesus' own teaching in Matthew 5:
23–24. The other element is one of acknowledging our
fellow worshipers as our brothers and sisters, as members

[1]Oscar Cullman, *Early Christian Worship,* London: SCM, 1959, pp. 19–20.
See also C. K. Barrett, *A Commentary on the Second Epistle to the Corinthians,*
New York: Harper & Row, 1973, p. 343.

of Christ's Body, and as God's own children. Jungmann especially stresses this aspect of the Peace. He notes that in Hippolytus the kiss is an acknowledgement of the newly consecrated bishop[2] and that the kiss of peace is confined to the faithful and indeed forbidden to be extended to the catechumens.[3] The kiss of peace then expresses our desire to "be in love and charity with our neighbors" and the acceptance of our fellow worshipers as our spiritual brothers and sisters, since they have not only been created by the one Father but also have been adopted as his children along with ourselves.

Here then are some good reasons for the Peace. Are they, however, as true now as in the time of the early church, when only believers were allowed to attend the Eucharist and when imperial persecution made sure that there were almost no merely nominal or only slightly committed Christians? We cannot be so sure that the person next to us in the pew is a baptized Christian, much less a committed one. Yet he or she cannot be sure of us either. Furthermore, in these days one's mere presence in church indicates some longing for God, some degree of self-exposure to him, some willingness (no matter how slight) to take the chance that God may use that moment of worship to touch one so deeply that he or she will never be the same again. We must take that neighbor on faith just as our neighbor must accept us. Doing so may remind us that there is no worthiness apart from Christ, either for us or for the other person. We cannot know whether our neighbor is a good Christian, but we cannot be sure of ourselves either. God, however, comes to us not because we deserve it nor because our merits are so evident. So

[2]Josef A. Jungmann, *The Early Liturgy*, London: Darton, Longman & Todd, 1959, p. 66.
[3]Ibid., p. 41.

with all the awkwardness of it, with all the uncertainty about what good it will do, both we and our neighbors can say, "The peace of the Lord be always with you." May our prayers help them and their prayers assist us; may God's peace find room in each of us.

4. In Your Infinite Love

*In your infinite love
you made us for yourself.*

Someone who lives in the shadow of Independence Hall may wonder why visitors gaze at the building in such a thoughtful way. It is so familiar that its impact is dimmed or nonexistent. The same thing happens with a truth that is so well-known that we never think of its meaning. That God created us may for most of us be one of those truths we know so well that the impact is lost, but the implications of this conviction are many and significant. Perhaps we can uncover some of these important consequences by pondering the question, "Did anyone ask if you wanted to be born?" Obviously, no one did. Suddenly one day there you were, abruptly thrust into life in the delivery room of a hospital. Though protesting vigorously, you had a life to live, whether you wished it or not. Who was responsible? Of course we answer, "Our parents." Yet are they the only ones involved? If so, they might enter a claim that they own certain rights over the life they alone have produced. In ancient society this theory was the prevailing one, and the newborn baby was brought in for the father's inspection. If he took the infant in his arms, the child was kept. If the father refused the child, because it was deformed or female or for any of a variety of reasons, the baby would be exposed to death on a lonely hillside or tossed into the Tiber.

Society today forbids such things and denies that the parents own the child. On what basis is this denial made? We ask where the parents gained this power to create a human life and perceive that they obtained this capacity from the human race. Hence society has some interest in the child and forbids the parents to act as though that little life were their exclusive possession. Is society, then, the possessor? A totalitarian society believes it is and therefore claims the right to dispose of any life which does not contribute to the welfare of the state. Our conscience rebels against this claim and rightly insists that we must ask where humanity gained the power of giving life. The source of life, God himself, is the ultimate giver of human existence, so that neither the parents nor the state owns us. Neither do we own ourselves. Life is not our own achievement; it is a gift from God.

Ultimately God the Creator is responsible for the fact that you found yourself with the gift of life on your hands. Yet what kind of gift is this one? Life is a wonderful thing but also a rather awesome affair. Without this unchosen fact of life, what glorious experiences we would have missed. Without it we would never have known what it is like to love or to be loved, would never have known the comfort of a familiar voice or the tonic effect of a cheer, would never have felt the satisfaction of a job well done or the spirit-lifting power of a cheerful song. Unknown would have been the sweetness of a peach, the crunch of an apple, the warmth of the sun, or the coolness of water from a hidden spring. The gift of life makes possible our feeling the calmness of a northern lake as the sun sets behind the dark pines, the persistent motion of the waves on a sandy beach, or the startling change brought by the first snowfall of the season. The gift of life is a wonderful thing, but it is also a bit frightening. Suddenly there you are, a fighting little creature with a life to live, and that is a sobering thought. It is not only that life contains rattle-snakes as well as peaches, criticism as well as cheers, and hate as well as love. It is also that each person has a life story to write, an autobiography to create. What kind of story will it be? Will it be a tale of achievement or of wasted chances, of nobility or of meanness, of courage or of petty cowardice, of concern for others or of unlovely selfishness, of humanity or of inhumanity? The doctor says the baby cries because it is getting its lungs working, and he is right. Yet there are reasons why an old poet might claim that the baby's wails mean something more. The gift of life is wonderful, but it is frightening too.

How much is meant, then, by the words, "In your infinite love you made us for yourself." Despite the terrifying responsibility of being so unceremoniously thrust into life, we acknowledge that love lies behind the gift. The wonders of life are to be enjoyed, and we give thanks for them. We accept the responsibility of a life history with confidence that, since love began it, love desires the history to be a worthwhile thing and will help to make it such. That same love is ceaselessly at work also to make the painful parts of life contribute in some fashion to the triumphant end of the tale, even though we cannot see how God can do it. We did not ask to be alive, and sometimes we wonder if there is any reason why we are. When we say these words of the Consecration Prayer, we are in effect asserting, "I believe that Love gave me a life, I believe there is a point to this life, and so I can live it with some assurance and some trust."

You made us

The belief that God made us also tells us something about ourselves. The Genesis account reads "So it was; and God saw all that he had made, and it was very good" (Gen. 1:31a). Bluntly, since God created you, you are worth something. Other persons may tell us we are worthless and we may feel that way too, but God does not agree. We are accustomed to hearing sermons on the perils of pride, and those warnings are needed. Human pride has left a long trail of wreckage in the history of mankind, but many other lives have been crippled by the opposite error. A feeling of worthlessness and inferiority yields a wretched harvest of resentment, self-pity, and hate. To get rid of one demon by inviting in another one is never helpful.

There are dramatically talented persons in the world, people who shine and sparkle and glow. If we are not like that, it is so easy to feel we have been cheated. Our talents are less noticeable ones, and so we neglect their development or even come to forget their existence. How few human beings, however, really do all they can with the gifts they possess? Were we to develop fully the talents we have, assuredly we would end in praising the Creator rather than resenting him. It was in his *infinite* love that he made us, and we need to ponder the word "infinite." It certainly suggests the astounding variety of the Creator's work. From him there come both elephants and butterflies, both steam and ice, both oak trees and daisies, both ostriches and hummingbirds. In creating people he shows the same wonderful gift of variety, and each of us is a variation that he wants. To accept oneself is not arrogance but humility; for your unique self is something God intended, and he made no duplicates.

The infinite nature of his creating love also reminds us that he is full of surprises. What he will finally make of a human life is more than we can predict. St. Paul turned out to be a good bit of a surprise to those who knew him as a youth, and indeed Paul himself must have been startled too. The prophet said, "For since the beginning of the world men have not heard, nor perceived by the ear, neither hath the eye seen, O God, beside thee, what he had prepared for him that waiteth for him" (Is. 64:4). The wonders God has in store for us include not only what he will do *for* us but also what he can do *with* us. It has been said that the way to make people hopeless is to treat them as such. We can treat ourselves in the same devastating manner, but no creator likes to see his handiwork scorned. He made us, so there must be something worthwhile for us to do and to become.

For yourself

Every employer has had an employee whose services were indispensable but whom he simply could not like as a person. You cannot do without his skills and expertise, you reward him handsomely, but you spend as little time with him as possible. Perhaps some have had the experience of being that indispensable but unloved individual. We know we are needed and that our work is highly valued, but we also know that we ourselves are not very welcome. No matter how great the rewards we can command, we still feel some resentment. It is one thing to be wanted because we can produce, and it is a very different thing to be wanted also because we are ourselves. It does matter, therefore, to know that God made us for himself. He cares about us, not just about what we accomplish nor even what we become. There are two reasons for our believing this truth, a negative and a positive one. Negatively, God does not need us; he created us because he loves us. It is possible for us to imagine that God has to have us around, because he needs someone to love. Yet one of the practical implications of the doctrine of the Trinity is that this assertion is not true. The Father has someone to love, namely the Son, and vice versa. Hence, he created us not because he needed us but because he loves us.

Positively, we have the explicit teaching of God's Son. Jesus quite clearly assures us that he and the Father desire our companionship in eternity. He has said:

There are many dwelling-places in my Father's house; if it were not so I should have told you; for I am going there on purpose to prepare a place for you. And if I go and prepare a place for you, I shall come again and receive you to myself, so that where I am you may be also. (Jn. 14:2–3)

He desires to receive us not only in heaven but to himself. He desires us to be where he is, and that place is "in the bosom of the Father" (Jn. 1:18). God seeks not just our obedience or our works or our worship; he seeks us. The greatest as well as the simplest definition of heaven is given by Paul when he writes, "Then we who are left alive shall join them, caught up in clouds to meet the Lord in the air. Thus we shall always be with the Lord" (I Th. 4:17). We want to be with him; the wonderful truth is that God wishes the same thing for us. He created us for nothing less.

Prayer is more than sending messages up to God and receiving directions and answers back from him. Essentially it is a matter of being with him, and he wants that even more than we do. The Eucharist is more than a receiving of forgiveness and guidance and strength. It is basically receiving him, a matter of Jesus coming to be with us. He has promised, "I will not leave you orphans" (Jn. 14:18). The deepest ache we know is loneliness, but the Father desires us to be with him in this life and in eternity. In his infinite love he made us, not to be useful to him nor to satisfy any whim for mere variety. He made us for himself.

5. And When We Had Fallen

And when we had fallen into sin and
become subject to evil and death.

The word "subject" leaps out of these lines to command attention. We are proud of our freedom, and we sturdily claim that we are not subject to anyone or anything. We therefore squirm when Jesus says, "In very truth I tell you, that everyone who commits sin is a slave" (Jn. 8:34). The very fact that we resist so much suggests that there may here be an uncomfortable truth that we need to examine. The word "subject" suggests captivity, helplessness, a lack of freedom. So we protest that we are not slaves of sin, insist that we can avoid sinning if we just try a little harder. Is not this idea of subjection just some more of that customary exaggeration employed by the clergy to make a point clear enough?

Honesty compels us to admit that there is such a thing as captivity to evil. There are men and women who once drank more than they should have but who, at some un-perceived stage along the road, have crossed over into a state in which they can no longer take any alcohol at all without being caught in the grip of an uncontrollable monster. Some others once freely began to experiment with drugs and now are addicted and bound fast in chains of their own forging. They are now victims, captives to whom earnest appeals to try harder are nothing less than mockery. To describe them as "subject" is certainly not an exaggeration.

Yet what of the rest of us, we who are not (or at least not yet) in any such state? Plain truth does raise the disquieting thought that these captive brothers and sisters of ours were also loudly insisting not long ago that they "could take it or leave it," when in reality they had already passed over that unperceived dividing line. Truth also notes that envy or self-pity or hatred or vengefulness can become an obsession too, can be so long entertained in a person's mind that it turns from a guest in the house to the master of the house. When does the habit of complaining or criticizing or boasting become so firmly entrenched that resolutions of changing mean nothing at all? It can happen to human beings, and it has.

Yet again we protest that these instances are dramatic and unusual ones, not truly applicable to average people like us. In reply the preacher can cite St. Paul, "The good which I want to do, I fail to do; but what I do is the wrong which is against my will" (Rom. 7:19). Now we may feel that this approach is a typical clergyman's trick, quoting a text and imagining that the argument is therefore ended. Yet before we cry "Foul," let us pause to consider. Paul did truly "try harder"; he went after everything in a fierce way. He did throw himself into the pursuit of a noble life, and he was not the kind of man who easily admitted defeat. The power of evil is both subtle and pervasive. Is there any human being who has not found that he or she began some project with all the best intentions and then, somewhere along the road, self-interest slipped in and distorted an honest attempt at goodness? Have we not seen how leaders of good causes have become involved in power struggles for top posts and how some have withdrawn when they were not given the credit they felt they deserved? Yet so often they did not intend to act that way, and in many instances they did not recognize the pattern of their behavior. What happened to them can also befall us. Evil can be very subtle, and even the best intentions cannot prevent its infiltration.

Evil is pervasive, as well as subtle, and no one is free from its omnipresent effect. Even if we never ourselves add to the sorry tale of racial discrimination, racism exists in society. We genuinely protest that we did not cause it, that we deplore it and wish it removed. For example, a corporation may be guilty of racial discrimination. Perhaps we are employees of that company, but we are not on the board of directors. Or perhaps we own two shares of stock, left us in grandfather's will, and voting two shares will not change anything. Or maybe we have a life insurance policy with a company that owns a large block of that corporation's stock. Or perhaps we only buy a gallon of gasoline made by a company which uses a chemical additive manufactured by the guilty corporation. We resent it when someone calls us racists because our involvement is so tangential and so involuntary. In frustration we protest, "That is not my fault; I cannot escape from a society of such complexity." And that is just the point. We cannot escape; we are subject. Evil is more than we can handle by ourselves.

We are not only entangled in a world that is bent; we are also contributors to the wrongness of it all. Day after day we are influenced by a psychological barrage of motivations that are unchristian or less than Christian. Incredible diligence, self-perception, and strength would be needed to resist that relentless pressure, and rare indeed is the person who accomplishes it. We call them saints, and they tell us that they could not have done it by themselves. They insist that God did it in them and through them. We really are compelled to admit that we are subject, even though the admission comes hard. Yet the essential first step to being rescued is accepting the fact of subjection. If we gladly think of Jesus as teacher but really do not feel he is our Savior, the probable reason is that we have not yet realized that we need to be rescued, that we cannot do it by ourselves, that just trying harder will not be enough. In fact we were subject, and it was for our rescue that Jesus came.

Subject . . . to death

Yet even when we have been brought to admit that we became subject to evil, we may find it hard to accept the statement that we also became subject to death. We are aware that death is seen by many as a necessary aspect of evolution, and we therefore have trouble with the biblical idea of death as the result of human sin. Has not the human race always been subject to death, quite apart from sin? The ancient rabbis pointed out that in the Garden of Eden there existed the Tree of Life, and from this fact they concluded that man was potentially immortal before his sin removed that possibility. Let us not be too quick to dismiss this reply as just some more biblical fundamentalism. If man had not sinned at all but had developed fully and completely his potential, how quickly would the goal of evolution have been reached? If that question seems too abstract, let us recast it and ask ourselves what the human race would be like now if there had been no sin in the past? How different would this world be if there had never been any wars, any slave traders, any plunderers of natural resources, or any despots? The world would be a very different place, and the human race would be vastly more advanced. The goal of evolution might have been reached a long time ago.

Another understanding of the Genesis story, however, might be reasonably suggested. Man worked in the Garden before the Fall, tending the garden. His work was a happy affair, and the Fall did not cause work to be necessary but to become confused and frustrated. The character of work did not change, but man's attitude toward it was corrupted. Just so, it might be suggested, was man's relation to death made wrong. Death is the moment when a man's life is surrendered back to the Creator, an abandonment of the self into the hands of him who created initially and can also recreate the transformed resurrection body of which St. Paul speaks. Had there been no sin, would we find this self-abandonment to God so difficult and so painful? Perhaps we fear to entrust ourselves to him simply because we have been so untrustworthy in our dealings with him and with others. Since we have so repeatedly been faithless creatures, we find it hard to believe that the Creator continues to be faithful. Under these circumstances death has a very different meaning, and we must acknowledge that we have become subject to that kind of death and need to be rescued from it.

Yet we are subject to death not only in that we are captive to it, however, it may be described, but also in that we have become its agents. Sin kills, and we as sinners have done a lot of destroying. The slave ships of the seventeenth and eighteenth centuries, the sweat shops of the nineteenth, and the concentration camps of the twentieth —these alone are evidence of how sin kills. Perhaps we have not shared in such horrors. Yet what of the happiness of a child damaged by a sarcastic remark, or the creativity of an artist stunted by the contempt visited upon his first painting? How many timid persons have we walked over, how many shy ones have we brushed aside, and how many trusting ones have we betrayed? In our busyness we have failed to hear many a cry for help, and in our self-concern we have sailed past many a drowning person. We need to be rescued from the death-dealing power of sin which not only makes us captives but also accessories in our own and others' captivity.

6. You, In Your Mercy

You, in your mercy, sent Jesus Christ,
your only and eternal Son, to share our human nature,
to live and die as one of us.

Here we are, then, subject to sin and to death. We have entangled ourselves in nets of our own weaving, and the more we thrash around the more thoroughly we are caught. But God, in his mercy, cares and he cares enough to become involved himself. He does not just send some form of rescue; he himself does the saving. Perhaps we might think, "Yes, but the Father sends the Son to do it rather than coming himself." Yet such a thoroughgoing separation of the Father and Son can be deceiving. Any parent, even a self-absorbed one, knows that it often hurts more to watch his or her child suffer than to bear the pain in place of the child. How often a parent stands by the side of a sick son or daughter and says, "I'd rather be there myself and take my child's place." How many say it, and mean it with absolute sincerity. Indeed one of the parent's greatest hurts is the awareness that it cannot be done.

The Son comes to save us, and he does so by entering into our state. There is more than one reason why he acts in this fashion and more than one significance to be found in it. Surely, however, one very important consequence for us is the fact that this strange method assures us that

God really understands us. One of the great verses of Scripture is Hebrews 4:15, "For ours is not a high priest unable to sympathize with our weaknesses, but one who, because of his likeness to us, has been tested every way, only without sin." Jesus Christ understands, because he has been where we are. He came "to live and die as one of us," a truth to be considered later. We can benefit, however, by looking also at the truth that he came "to share our human nature."

One of our problems is the pain that can come upon us in the course of life, but another source of difficulty is the fact that we are human. It is not easy to partake of human nature, that wonderful but perplexing mixture. We are animals, but more than animals; we are not angels, but we are at once both less and potentially more than angels. What problems are posed for us simply because we are human? Because we are human, we can be less than human and false to our humanity, a peril no animal faces. A rabbit is just a rabbit; it can be neither more nor less. A rabbit does not have to puzzle over what is required to be a true rabbit; it just is one. Not so, however, for the human creature. Otherwise there would not be such a multitude of books on the subject of what it is to be truly human. Again, we are all familiar with the phrase, "man's inhumanity to man," but we never talk about "the rabbit's un-rabbitness to rabbits." We can be less than human; we can live as swine, as worms, or as parasites. There is nothing wrong when a pig is a pig, a worm is a worm, or a fungus is a fungus, but there is something wrong when a human being is less than human. This burden Jesus understands, because he shared it.

Another characteristic of human nature is the possession of intelligence, which is also a mixed blessing. We can see ahead in ways an animal cannot, and so we can pursue long-range joys and avoid future dangers. This capacity, however, can bring pain as well as joy. Our intellect can foresee potential perils ahead but cannot see with equal clarity how those possible dangers can be met. Hence the very human tendency to cross bridges before we reach them, even though experience has so often taught us that many feared bridges never do appear on our road. Even when the forecast is correct and the trouble does arrive on schedule, we have worn ourselves out by fussing about it before we could begin to handle it. Someone has said that anxiety is the gap between our ability to foresee possible evils and our trust that the evils can be met and overcome. If we were too stupid to envision trouble, or so trusting that we did not fear it, life would be much easier. Of course Jesus teaches:

Set your mind on God's kingdom and his justice before everything else, and all the rest will come to you as well. So do not be anxious about tomorrow; tomorrow will look after itself. Each day has troubles enough of its own. (Mt. 6:33–34)

Since we cannot throw away the double-edged sword of intelligence, the approach Jesus advises is the only solution. The point to be stressed here, however, is that his teaching us about the problem shows that he understands it.

A third aspect of human nature is a certain degree of freedom of will. We are free to accept, or to refuse to accept, God's sovereignty. We are free to accept his love or to reject it, because love by its very nature must be unforced. At first glance this fact might seem to be an unmixed thing, something easy to take or easy to refuse. Yet that conclusion is quite false. At first it would seem very easy to reject God's love for us, since he will not impose it on us. Neither will he vengefully punish us for rejecting him; for he sends the rain upon the field of the just and the unjust alike. It must be easy to refuse him, because so many human beings do just that. Yet is it really so, when we look more closely? We are made for love, created to love and to be loved. If it were not so, we would not discover that loneliness is one of the cruelest hurts that we can experience. So we seek to love others and get them to love us, imagining that this attempt may solve the problem and leave us content without God's love. But it does not work, or at least it does not work well enough. The experience of loving and of being loved is indeed wonderful, but there is still that something more we keep desiring. We may not know what it is or why we want it, but we detect the ring of truth in St. Augustine's words, "Our hearts are restless 'till they find their home in thee."

This truth is not a downgrading of human love; on the contrary it glorifies human love as both springing from and leading to the Creator of love. The artist sees beauty and so is led on to the search for even greater beauty, and the taste of love has the same effect. If we do not allow this leading onward to occur, we fall back on human love and demand that it accomplish more than it can. To demand that a marriage meet an eternal need is to expect your mate to take God's place, and that is asking too much. We expect superhuman loving, resent it when our partner fails to meet the unrealistic demand, and then start to destroy the love that was all we knew.

So, we may conclude, let us accept God's love, since that is easy. After all love does not demand anything; instead it seeks to give. Of course it is true that God's love is not given on a conditional basis, that he does not promise to love us if we behave properly, obey enough, and bow down frequently enough. He does not require us to earn his love; he just loves and indeed loves first. How then could the acceptance of his love be anything but easy? He is not demanding, but accepting love makes us demand things of ourselves. When someone loves us and we welcome the love, then we wish to be more worthy of that love. We want to be the finest person we can become, for the sake of the one who loves us.

God also wishes us to be our finest selves, and all his commands have this end in view. Yet he wishes this growth not for his own sake, but for our happiness. Again Jesus says, "If you love me you will obey my commands; and I will ask the Father, and he will give you another to be your Advocate, who will be with you for ever—the Spirit of truth" (John 14:15–16). He does not teach that our obedience earns the gift of the Spirit nor that our disobedience will lead God to withhold the Spirit. Rather, the disobedient man will shrink from God and refuse the Spirit's coming. Accepting God's love does get us involved in trying to obey the divine commands, but only because we want to do so. In truth we do not have any easy way out. It is not easy either to accept his love or to reject it. This dilemma is part of being human, and Jesus understands it. He came "to share our human nature," and he knows what it is like to be that strange and yet marvelous mixture, a human being.

To live and die as one of us

As Jesus shares our lot, he not only partakes of human nature in some general sort of way, but he experiences the same things we do and in the same fashion. He lives, and dies, as we do. The way we live is the same way he lived on earth. He must have enjoyed life as we enjoy it or he could not have created the parables he told. He must have taken pleasure in seeing flowers grow in the fields and foxes slip into their dens, observing women making bread and fathers dealing with prodigal or proper sons, and watching the rain fall on every man's fields with a wonderfully indiscriminate generosity. Yet life, as we know it, includes pain as well as joy. Does Jesus understand that too?

Jesus knows what pain is, because he felt it too. He experienced physical pain when he was flogged and crucified, and it was excruciating pain. Yet he also learned what it was like to be weary, to be so pressed upon by others that there was not time for a decent meal, and to be afflicted with thirst. Neither is he a stranger to other human hurts; for he knows what it is to be deserted by friends when the going gets tough, to be betrayed by a trusted companion, and to be jeered at by enemies. He learned how it feels to be distrusted and misunderstood by one's own family, and he tasted the bitterness of being rejected by those one seeks to help. He lived as one of us, and so he shared the pains which come upon us.

Since he lived as we live, Jesus also understands the problems we face as creatures who live in time. We are troubled not only by the prospect of danger and pain, but also by the long wait until the difficulty comes before we can deal with it. How often have we cried, "I would just like to get it over with." Jesus said essentially the same thing: "I have a baptism to undergo, and how hampered I am until the ordeal is over!" (Lk. 12:50). Something of the same pressure was evident when he said to Judas, "Do quickly what you have to do" (Jn. 13:27). Since we live in time, we suffer because we do not know when something will happen or how long it will be until we see the fruits of our efforts. Jesus understands this burden, since he said,

"But about that day or that hour no one knows, not even the angels in heaven, not even the Son; only the Father" (Mk. 13:32). Human beings must live in the stream of time, but our High Priest knows how it feels.

Jesus not only lived as we do, he also died as we shall. It is not just that he died but that he died as a human being does. One of the devastating things about death, as we envisage it, is our helplessness to prevent it. We are clever and inventive, and we have succeeded so often in avoiding certain pains, escaping certain perils, and turning some disasters into triumphs. But here is something we cannot escape and cannot control. We are helpless, and we fear and resent being that way. Jesus too was unable to escape death, unless he were to betray his commission to be and to speak the truth. He could have commanded legions of angels to destroy those who schemed against him, slapped him and spat on him, shoved him along the way to Golgotha and nailed him to the cross. He was not helpless in that sense, but he was even more bitterly helpless. He could not force men to believe and repent and cease their self-destructive march into darkness. Love must be invited and not forced, and he was helpless before that truth.

Another aspect of dying which afflicts us is the undignified nature of it. For so many there is the indignity of being ignored as too old and of being dependent on others for even the simplest needs. Then comes the moment of death when our terrible fragility and our mere creatureliness become so very evident. The incisive man who built an industrial empire, the beautiful woman whose charm could cajole anyone into doing anything, the impressive individual whose personality was so commanding that everyone obeyed without asking why—for each there comes such indignity. The same was true for Jesus. We look back at the Crucifixion as an heroic event, seeing the martyr's steadfastness and the Savior's perfect love. Yet did it look that way when it happened? There was indignity in fullest measure for God's only-begotten Son. It could not have been an impressive and solemn scene of heroism, or we would not read of the crowd's mockery and the sneering remarks of the chief priests and the scribes, "He saved others; himself he cannot save." He died as we do, with no support save trust in the love and power of the Father. He died as one of us that we might die as he did, crying "Father, into thy hands I commend my spirit." He has shared our condition, and he knows what it is like to be a human being.

7. To Reconcile Us

To reconcile us to you,
the God and Father of all.

To reconcile one party to another means to have the first party abandon its enmity and anger toward the other. Who is angry with whom, in the relationship between God and sinful man? Scripture insists that we are hostile to him, rather than the opposite. We need to be reconciled to God, not God to us. How can this be, when we are the ones who transgressed? Our psychologist friends can help us understand by their description of the typical guilt reaction. If one of us spreads a malicious tale about a neighbor, what happens next? We see him coming down the street toward us, and we look for a side street down which we can duck to avoid meeting him. Perhaps he has found out that we are the guilty person and we are afraid of being rebuked. Even if he has not yet found out, we still feel uncomfortable and so wish to avoid him. Then there comes the next stage. We do not like to feel uncomfortable, and so we unconsciously seek some reason to claim that he hurt us first so we were justified in what we did to him. Whether the claim is exaggerated or wholly unreal, we still must find some reason. So we convince ourselves that it is really his fault, not ours; he is the guilty one, not we.

With God we do the same thing. The story of Adam neatly illustrates the process. It is Adam who hides behind those bushes, not God. When faced with his guilt, Adam first seeks to put the blame on Eve. Yet he then goes further by saying, "The woman *you gave* to be with me, she gave me of the tree, and I did eat." God made the woman, and so it is really God's fault, not Adam's. We do the same thing today. We blame it on someone else, on our parents, on our upbringing, on society, on anybody or anything other than ourselves. Furthermore, it is God's fault, since he created us and put us in a world such as this one, where all kinds of temptation lie around us. If he had made us angels or put us in a perfect world, we would never have done anything wrong. It is all his fault, and we tell ourselves that we have a right to be angry with him.

How does God's sending of his Son change the situation and reconcile us to the Father? For one thing it frees us from the fear of having him find out that we are guilty. He already knows, and that is why he sent the Son. As St. Paul puts it, "Christ died for us while we were yet sinners" (Rom. 5:8a). There is more to it than only the fear of being found out, but that element is important. Fear always arouses hate, while removing the fear eases the need to hate. God already knows all about us, and we have nothing more we need try to hide from him. Also, the sending of the Son proves that God loves us and does not hate us.

Here is the second point, that God knows all we have done and yet loves us. He believes we are worth loving. In our guilt we find it hard not to hate ourselves and so are sure the injured One must also hate us. The sending of the Son proves that he does not hate us, so we do not have to hate ourselves. His anger is directed not toward us but toward the sin that hurts us as well as it damages others. We have already glanced at the truth that we are the victims of sin as well as the instruments of it. Guilt always provokes hate, so it is important to direct the enmity toward the right object. Our hatred should be aimed at sin, not at ourselves nor at God. To see how God aims his "anger" can help us learn how rightly to direct our own.

The third point is that God does something about the sin; he does not simply lament it. He summons us to join in this struggle against sin and to stop wasting time and energy by hating ourselves or hating him. We share in the fight by repentance and amendment; we are his partners in the effort, reconciled to him and at peace with God, who calls us to be his allies and not his enemies.

The God and Father of all

Is guilt, however, the only reason for our failure to be at peace with God? Of course we shy away from saying that we are angry at God, because of an instinctive fear that some calamity would be hurled upon us if we said, or even thought, anything like that. Yet self-honesty may lead some to admit that such a feeling is really theirs. We human beings may indeed feel angry with God because of some burden we bear or some pain we experience. Perhaps it is a congenital illness or a birth defect, perhaps that our family background was an unhappy or underprivileged one, or perhaps that we are members of a minority group that is the object of scorn and prejudice. It may be that one of us has been made to feel his life was cramped because he was not raised in a family whose sons went to Harvard, and so he could not count on family friends to open doors of opportunity in business or government or a profession. For someone else it may be resentment that her sister was attractive, popular, and fashionably slim, while so many thought she was plain that she came to believe she really was unattractive. For someone else it may be the feeling that he is trapped in a dead-end job or an unhappy marriage, or the feeling that his life is a lonely thing. Whatever the cause, many a person secretly thinks that God has been unfair, that he may be a loving Father for others but not for himself or herself. How does the sending of Christ bring such beings to peace with God?

First, Jesus shows that our burdens are not God-given punishments. He comes to save, not to deliver lectures on how fitting and just our sufferings are. In fact he several times denies quite specifically that we can equate suffering and sin. When they meet a man blind from birth, the disciples ask, "Rabbi, who sinned, this man or his parents?" (John 9:2). Jesus replies, "Neither." Again we read:

At that very time there were some people present who told him about the Galileans whose blood Pilate had mixed with their sacrifices. He answered them: "Do you imagine that, because these Galileans suffered this fate, they must have been greater sinners than anyone else in Galilee? I tell you they were not; but unless you repent, you will all of you come to the same end. Or the eighteen people who were killed when the tower fell on them at Siloam—do you imagine they were more guilty than all the other people living in Jerusalem? I tell you they were not; but unless you repent, you will all of you come to the same end." (Lk. 13:1–5)

What Jesus teaches in words he also declares in actions. He cleanses the lepers, heals the sick, and makes the lame walk; he does not tell them they deserve what happened to them. If the Father had intended those sufferings as punishment for sin, the perfectly obedient Son would not have set those men and women free from their afflictions. So we, in our sufferings, are first led to see that our resentment and bitterness and hate are misplaced. We are blaming God for something he has not done.

Yet can nothing more be said? It helps to see that God did not do it, but then we need to ask whether he does or does not care about these pains. So the second point is that the sending of the Son shows that God does care, in fact he cares deeply. He is so concerned that he gets involved in the hurt and the agony of mankind. As the Incarnate Son, God shared the whole mess. As we have already seen, the Son shared our human nature, lived and died as one of us. Yet Jesus Christ not only *shared* our lot; he *shares* it now. By baptism we are brought to live in him while he comes to live in us. He lives in us, prays in us, laughs in us, and also hurts in us. Everyone has sometime felt that surge of resentment when someone says, "I know how you feel." You bite your tongue lest you should blurt out, "No, you don't, because you are not where I am." Yet Jesus Christ can truly say it, because he has so identified himself with us.

Even more important, however, is the third truth, that God sends the Son to do something about these human pains. Jesus does not theorize about the source of evil; he leads the attack against the evil that twists human lives. He does more than rescue individual victims by cleansing lepers and making the lame walk, by casting out demonic forces, and by bringing truth to the banishment of falsehood and ignorance. He goes down into the valley of death to grapple decisively with the very power of evil itself. Of course the battle takes a very strange form, crucifixion and then resurrection. We find it hard to understand that astounding method, and even Christ cried out,

"My God, why?" If Jesus cried out that way, the hurt and confused man or woman who blurts out the same question will not be condemned. Yet it must be noted that Jesus' agonized question received no intellectual answer; the answer was the divine act of Easter. It is not an Easter message but an Easter event. God takes the terrible wrong of Jesus' murder and makes it the instrument of man's salvation. The evil thing is not explained, but rather it is transformed. How complete is this way of defeating evil. The wrong is not just prevented, not just overcome; it is turned into a springboard to a greater good.

From this essential revelation of God's way of working we can learn his intent with our afflictions too. He seeks ever to transform them into good, if we will allow him to work and will stop interfering with the process. St. Paul tells us so when he writes, "He pleads for God's own people in God's own way; and in everything, as we know, he cooperates for good with those who love God and are called according to his purpose" (Rom. 8:28). Sometimes we can catch a glimpse of how he does it, with human cooperation. For example, a man becomes ill, is confined to bed for some time, is forced to stop rushing about, and accepts the grace to ask where he is rushing and why. For the first time in many years he is face to face with himself, prevented from taking his customary path of escaping from thought by plunging into further activity. He begins to ask himself some unwelcome questions, "What am I looking for; what point is there to my life; is a possible promotion worth the neglect of my family and the courting of an early death; can I stand being with myself for a moment here in time and for eternity hereafter; is my life an offering to God or a sacrifice on the altar of ambition or of psychological compulsion?" If he dares to ask those questions and permit the Spirit to bring him to honest answers, his life thereafter will be a much better thing for him and for others. The evil will have been turned into a source of good. Several things need to be noted. The evil event is not caused by God, but used by him. It is labeled a bad thing, and we are not expected to play semantic games and call it good. The possible benefit is not automatic; our cooperation is required to assist in the transformation that divine mercy is working to achieve.

At times we can perceive how God brings good out of evil, as in the illustration just offered. At other times we cannot perceive it and must honestly state that we do not see how even God could do anything good with this particular evil which has befallen us or someone else. It does matter, however, to be assured that he is at work to transform the terrible thing, even though we may not understand how he did it until eternity lets us perceive the things now hidden from us. This assurance, given by a faith which at times is painfully blind, can make possible that peace with God that seems so unlikely. On rare occasions we may meet someone who has won through to such a faith, who has found that kind of confidence in the face of great temptation to resent God. Such a person has been reconciled to God and has accepted the truth that he is the Father of all. Such serenity we find amazing, but we also discover that it is most attractive. That serenity can be ours when we learn that God is the Father of all, including us.

To be reconciled to God means to be at peace with him. If in our hearts there is resentment, the feeling that he has been unfair to us, the first step is to admit to ourselves that we do indeed feel that way. God knows our feelings, and he sent the Son to reconcile us to himself. The gift of his Son assures us that the Father does not hate us, that he believes we are worth loving, that our afflictions are not a tit-for-tat retaliation for our sins, that he cares about our hurts, and that he is ever active to bring good out of everything that happens to us. We seemingly persist in asking why things happen, but he seems more concerned to do something with those events, and something good. As we come to believe that truth and are occasionally given a glimpse of its actuality, we grow into peace with God. We need that kind of peace; for only when there is peace with God can we have peace with others and within ourselves.

8. He Stretched Out His Arms

He stretched out his arms upon the cross,
and offered himself, in obedience to your will,
a perfect sacrifice for the whole world.

"He stretched out his arms" throughout his time here on earth; he stretched them out to embrace poor, blind, stumbling men and women whose pain called out his compassion. It was into those arms he took the little children when he blessed them, and those arms were extended when he touched the lepers and made them clean. When he looked with pity at the self-doomed city of Jerusalem, he said, "O Jerusalem, Jerusalem, the city that murders the prophets and stones the messengers sent to her! How often have I longed to gather your children, as a hen gathers her brood under her wings; but you would not let me" (Lk. 13:34). As he wished to gather the people of Jerusalem, so he wished to gather all men into his loving embrace, but mankind would not allow it. So those arms designed for protective encircling are instead stretched out, and stretched out upon the cross.

Love is helpless in the face of refusal; the loving one must wait until the love is welcomed. The pain of that truth is well known to many a lover and to many a parent. No one feels quite so helpless as one who must stand and watch a loved one get into trouble while all advice, love, and help are refused. It is just that kind of helplessness that the divine Love experienced at Golgotha. Today it is the same. Just so long as we refuse to allow his arms to embrace us, so long must his arms be stretched out—upon the cross.

He offered himself . . . a perfect sacrifice

When we think of a sacrifice, we tend to emphasize the death aspect of it. Yet the fundamental element of a sacrifice is the offering, not the dying. Had there been no sin at all, there would still have been the need for man to offer himself to God. Why so? Man must offer himself to God in order to be what he is and also to become what he is destined to become. Man is a created being, and to be true to his own nature he must acknowledge his Creator. Yet it is just this acknowledgment that man finds hard to make. As St. Paul expresses it,

For all that may be known of God by men lies plain before their eyes; indeed God himself has disclosed it to them. His invisible attributes, that is to say his everlasting power and deity, have been visible, ever since the world began, to the eye of reason, in the things he has made. There is therefore no possible defence for their conduct; knowing God, they have refused to honour him as God, or to render him thanks. (Rom. 1:19–21a)

Again Paul writes, "Thus, because they have not seen fit to acknowledge God, he has given them up to their own depraved reason. This leads them to break all rules of conduct" (Rom. 1:28). To acknowledge God as my Creator requires the admission that I am a creature; to confess him as God labels me as less than divine. Also, if God is my

Creator, then my life is not my own, to do with as I please. My life comes from him, and I must account to him for my use or misuse of it. Furthermore, as a dependent creature, I must look to the Creator not only for the beginning of my existence but also for its continuation and for the realization of the potential within me. I must offer myself to God in thanksgiving for my creation and also in obedience to God's intentions for my future. It is not sin that causes man's need to offer himself to God; this need has been there from Creation. As man, Jesus Christ makes the offering men and women need to make but find impossible to do alone.

Perhaps a little more light can be shed on this matter by asking what Jesus offers and when. Scripture tells us, "How much greater is the power of the blood of Christ; he offered himself without blemish to God, a spiritual and eternal sacrifice; and his blood will cleanse our conscience from the deadness of our former ways and fit us for the service of the living God" (Heb. 9:14). Again we read, "But as it is, he has appeared once and for all at the climax of history to abolish sin by the sacrifice of himself" (Heb. 9:26b). What Jesus offers is himself. Yet what makes up that self he offered? As a real human being, his self includes all of the things that happened to him, all of the experiences of his life. It includes Jesus' joy in looking at the flowers of the field, his interest in how the farmer sows his seed, and his sympathetic observation of how a shepherd seeks out a lost sheep and a father treats a prodigal son. Included too is his remarkable patience with Peter, his courageous debates with the Pharisees, his heartache at knowing that Judas would betray him and so betray himself, and his hopes for what would be achieved by that little band of awfully human disciples. All of these experiences are part of the self he offers to God, and this awareness may help us perceive that his sacrifice of himself involves his living and not simply his dying.

The same truth is clarified by asking when he offered himself in obedience to the Father's will. His obedience is a lifelong matter, not confined merely to the time of the Passion. The intent to obey was indeed the reason for his becoming man in the first place.

That is why, at his coming into the world, he says: "Sacrifice and offering thou didst not desire, But thou hast prepared a body for me. Whole-offerings and sin-offerings thou didst not delight in. Then I said, 'Here am I: as it is written of me in the scroll, I have come, O God, to do thy will.'" (Heb. 10:5–7)

He comes to be baptized by John in obedience to the Father's will, and in the Temptation he rejects any form of messianic ministry that is contrary to the Father's will. He can truthfully say to the disciples, "He who sent me is present with me, and has not left me alone; for I always do what is acceptable to him" (Jn. 8:29). The obedience of a lifetime lies behind Jesus' prayer in the Garden of Gethsemane, "Father, if it be thy will, take this cup away from me. Yet not my will but thine be done" (Lk. 22:42). His dying on Calvary is the completion in history of the obedient self-offering made by him at every moment of his life.

One reason for emphasizing this point is that we are summoned to offer ourselves, because of Christ's sacrifice and in union with it. St. Paul sums up our duty as Christians by writing, "Therefore, my brothers, I implore you by God's mercy to offer your very selves to him: a living sacrifice, dedicated and fit for his acceptance, the worship offered by mind and heart" (Rom. 12:1). His self-offering took the form of crucifixion because of the opposition of his enemies. Others, too, have been martyrs for the faith, and there may be more before the scroll of history is finally rolled. Yet for many the story has been a different one, and the self-offering asked of them has been not physical death but death to a way of living. Our task is not to dictate to the Father the form of offering we will make, but simply to offer ourselves in Christ with thanksgiving.

In obedience to your will . . . for the whole world

Yet we must still seek to understand why Jesus' self-offering took the form of death. Some attempts to explain the Crucifixion have seen the death as something the Father demanded of Christ as a satisfaction for the outrage of human sin. Of course any human attempt to understand a divine act is bound to fall short in some fashion, but the "satisfaction" theory of the cross is especially susceptible to being understood in a fashion which is not only inadequate but also distressing. It suggests a divergence of attitude between the Father and the Son, with the Father as a severe person whose demand for justice is contrasted with the loving Son's willingness to suffer on our behalf. Yet it is through Jesus Christ that we see the Father, and the nature of the Son is the truest clue to the nature of the Father. Father and Son are alike. Do we not then have to ask anew why the Son suffered and in what sense it was "in obedience to [his] will"?

Historically Jesus Christ died because evil men wanted him out of the way. Goodness is attractive as well as admirable, but goodness can also arouse violent antagonism in human hearts. Decidedly evil persons become upset when goodness threatens their scheming, and the high priests hated Jesus because he was a real danger to their moneymaking abuse of the Temple worship. Yet it is not just the blatantly evil who opposed him. Many who were more like us, a mixture of the mildly good and the unobtrusively sinful, also joined in crying "Crucify him." This fact should not surprise us. Over and over again human history has demonstrated that average folk welcome goodness in moderate doses but turn nasty when confronted by radical, thoroughgoing goodness. The reason is quite evident: in the presence of deep-down integrity we are made ashamed of our own measured, prudent, and careful goodness. The real thing exposes the virtue that is only partial. So we are driven to get rid of that clear godliness which makes us so uncomfortable. The goodness of Jesus was so bright that it made manifest the shadowy nature of human achievements, and the darkness sought to extinguish the light that was too strong.

Where then is the element of "obedience to [his] will"? It is in obedience to the Father's will that Jesus died, because the only way he could have avoided arousing man's deadly antagonism would have been by being less committed to the Father's cause, less incisive about the radical nature of goodness, and less honest about the ways in which the claims of God had been watered-down, adjusted, or even distorted. In a sinful world, goodness will be crucified. Jesus could not avoid that fate unless he became less than what the Father desired. In this sense his death is "in obedience to [his] will." At least thus far we can understand Christ's dying as something we human beings caused and not as a "pound of flesh" demanded by God to satisfy his sense of justice.

Yet have we said all that we can and must declare? Is this the only sense of the truth that he died in accordance with the Father's will? Assuredly not. We need also to recall the truth that sin brings death, that evil kills. It is obvious that hatred leads to murdering our brothers; it is less obvious, but equally true, that hatred kills something in the heart of the one who hates. Less obvious sins are also deadly. The potential creativity of a child is stunted or even destroyed by the contempt or the indifference of a parent or a teacher. Shy and tentative loving is crushed more than once when it is met by chilly self-absorption or brushed off by smug condescension. God, however, is the life giver. He does not kill; sin does. Yet if our sin makes us dead, we cannot offer ourselves to God. Somehow the destructive force of evil must be absorbed or we shall be destroyed. It is this deadly effect of sin which Jesus Christ accepts and takes into himself. The Father does not crucify the Son; men do, sin does. Jesus accepts it, and the Father permits it, because only thus can the destructive effects of evil be kept from killing the human beings God created and loved. Even in human experience we can perceive something of this process. When one person injures another and that other forgives, someone has to accept the pain and the hurt. The cross does just that on a cosmic scale, while the Resurrection demonstrates God's power even over evil. It is in this sense that Jesus died in accordance with the Father's will, for all mankind. The Father's intent, and the Son's intent, was the salvation of mankind, and the deadliness of sin had to be met in order to achieve that rescue.

This way of understanding the cross is not heretical and is in no way a watering-down of the truth that Jesus died in obedience to the Father's will. This approach makes clear that Jesus' death was more than an historical accident, more than just another example of martyrdom. The one who accepted death on Calvary was more than just another victim of human malice. He was God's only begotten Son, and his death had meaning for all of creation.

Furthermore, the intent of that martyr was a vastly greater one. He was not killed because his enemies took him by surprise, for "As the time approached when he was to be taken up to heaven, he set his face resolutely towards Jerusalem" (Lk. 9:51). He knew what would happen to him, for when warned about Herod's hostility he said, "It is unthinkable for a prophet to meet his death anywhere but in Jerusalem" (Lk. 13:33b). He did not die because he was a masochist who wished to suffer; in fact, he wished to have that cup taken from him if it were possible. Neither did he die because he was helpless against his enemies. He told Peter to sheathe his sword and cried, "Do you suppose that I cannot appeal to my Father, who would at once send to my aid more than twelve legions of angels?" (Mt. 26:53).

Why then did Jesus die? Jesus himself states that his death was necessary to rescue us from sin and its deadly results: "For even the Son of Man did not come to be served but to serve, and to surrender his life as a ransom for many" (Mk. 10:45). No single attempt to understand the cross and the Resurrection can be entirely adequate, for the human mind cannot fully grasp the actions of God. Yet this approach does fit with two important truths, the fact that sin is deadly and the fact that by the Passion Christ did for us something we could not do for ourselves. It also avoids the mistake of ascribing a very different character to the Father and to the Son. Both are motivated by love for mankind when the Son offers himself in obedience to the Father's will.

9. On the Night

> *On the night he was handed over to suffering and death,*
> *our Lord Jesus Christ took bread;*
> *and when he had given thanks to you,*
> *he broke it, and gave it to his disciples,*
> *and said, "Take, eat:*
> *This is my Body, which is given for you.*
> *Do this for the remembrance of me."*

What did Jesus intend when he gathered the disciples for the Last Supper? What did he mean by the things he did and the words he spoke there? It is important for us to know, as well as we can, and the very debates about his intentions reveal how much the issue has mattered to Christians down through the centuries. Surely one clue to his purposes is provided by the fact that it happened "on the night he was handed over to suffering and death." It happened at a particular time and so under a particular set of circumstances. The supper was held just before he was handed over, and the Gospels make it clear that Jesus knew at least to some degree what was about to befall him. He knew the hatred of his enemies had reached such an intensity that the storm would soon break. He knew that Jerusalem was the place where prophets were slain, and it was with this awareness that he had steadfastly set out to go there. He knew that Judas would betray him and that the other disciples would flee in fear. Loyalty to the Father's will and faithfulness to the task given him made it impossible for him to escape the fate he foresaw. The fact that he held the supper under these circumstances tells us something about what he meant.

Scholarly debates have swirled around the weight to be given to the fact that he *broke* the bread. Does that breaking symbolize sacrifice or not? The word "blood" used over the cup clearly implies sacrifice in any biblical setting, and so there have been arguments about whether he used that word or not. Yet the word "covenant" certainly involves a sacrifice motif, and almost no one questions the authenticity of that word. Yet there is even more evidence, whose cumulative weight is powerful indeed. Luke tells us that the disciples argued about "who among them should rank highest" (Lk. 22:24). It is most unlikely that Luke invented that tale, which presents the apostles in such an unappealing fashion. Of all times and all places in which such a wrangle should occur! The rather disgusting spectacle draws from Jesus the significant words, "But I am among you as one who serves" (Lk. 22:27). One does not have to be an expert biblical scholar to be reminded that in Scripture there is a great section about one who serves, the mysterious passages in Isaiah about the Suffering Servant. The haunting words are recalled:

> He was despised, he shrank from the sight of men,
>> tormented and humbled by suffering;
>> we despised him, we held him of no account,
>> a thing from which men turn away their eyes.
> Yet on himself he bore our sufferings,
>> our torments he endured,
> while we counted him smitten by God,
>> struck down by disease and misery;

but he was pierced for our transgressions,
   tortured for our iniquities;
the chastisement he bore is health for us
   and by his scourging we are healed. . . .
   So shall he, my servant, vindicate many,
   himself bearing the penalty of their guilt.
Therefore I will allot him a portion with the great,
   and he shall share the spoil with the mighty,
because he exposed himself to face death
   and was reckoned among transgressors,
because he bore the sin of many
   and interceded for their transgressions.

Is. 53:3–5, 11b–12

St. John tells us that Jesus washed the disciples' feet, girded with a towel in the manner of a servant. In St. Mark's gospel we learn that Jesus tried to teach the status-seeking disciples something of what he was and of what they therefore should be. He told them, "For even the Son of Man did not come to be served but to serve, and to give up his life as a ransom for many" (Mk. 10:45). Surely the meaning of the Last Supper must somehow be tied to the self-offering of Jesus, an offering he made "as a ransom for many." It was "on the night he was handed over to suffering and death" that Jesus took the bread and the cup; the meaning of his words and actions is connected with the setting in which it all took place.

This is my Body, which is given for you

As we try to understand the Last Supper, we must remember that it took place in the world of the Bible, not in the world of twentieth-century America. In the upper room a Jew of first-century Palestine was talking to other Jews of the same time, place, and culture. To know what he meant we need to get into the thought of that culture, and the Bible is our surest guide. Today many persons are puzzled by Jesus' words, "This is my Body." So they will ask, "How can he really mean that the broken bread is his body when he was still in his body when he spoke that way?" The question is a reasonable one, but Jesus and the disciples did not necessarily think exactly as we do.

We tend to think of a body as the physical part of the person. Conceivably, then, a person could exist without that one part, and we do not have much difficulty in understanding a Greek concept such as a soul existing without a body. Chapter 15 of First Corinthians shows clearly that St. Paul could not imagine existence, even heavenly existence, without some kind of body. Paul is a Jewish thinker, and we are therefore reminded that those Jews in the Upper Room did not think of a body as we do. In the biblical thought-world, a person does not *have* a body but *is* a body. The body is the self, the person, as an organized entity, as someone who can touch and be touched by persons and things outside himself or herself. Perhaps we can catch something of the difference by recalling that we ourselves say "Don't touch me." Notice that the speaker does not resent someone's touching a part of his self; he exclaims "Don't touch *me.*" That is, Do not touch my self. Earlier we noticed that what Jesus offers on the cross is himself, and at this point we might mention that it is not some part of himself but the whole self. It is hard to think as a first-century Jew did, but the effort is worthwhile. At least we can perceive that we are not being invited to engage in cannibalism. We can also see that our misunderstanding of the word "body" leads us to pose a question no one would have asked in the upper room. Christ is simply saying, over the bread, "This is me; this is my self." His self is present, and in that self the disciples can share.

Additional help comes from another fact. We cannot be entirely certain that Jesus added the words "which is given" when he spoke of the bread as his body, but we are quite sure that he did speak of the blood as that "which is shed for you." "Is shed" is a present participle. In Hebrew and Aramaic the present participle is used not only for the actual present but also for the immediate future. Jesus' blood historically was shed at the Crucifixion; his self-offering was in a temporal sense made on Golgotha and not in the Upper Room. Jesus bids the disciples to share in the self-offering he is about to make, to share in his obedient self which alone is an offering worthy to be presented to the Father. Morally the offering is already made, although temporally it will be made the next day. He set his face to Jerusalem, knowing what would happen. So he has already accepted his destiny; he has in will already offered himself. Therefore he can truly invite the disciples to share in his self-offering, even though his obedience must still be acted out in history, as the hours crawl past. The agony in Gethsemane, the refusal to find some escape during the trial before Pilate, and the Crucifixion itself must still be borne. Yet morally, as far as his will is concerned, he has already made the offering. With his will man has rejected God; the will of the Second Adam renders to the Father the obedience we need to offer. We are clearly concerned with the offering of self, and in biblical terms this is what "body" means.

One might then ask why Jesus did not say "self" instead of "body" and save us all this effort. Of course that request would ignore the fact of the Incarnation, the fact that he became man as a first-century Jew engaged in trying to

get his point across to other first-century Jews such as
Peter and James and John. Yet there is an added value for
us in that he did use the word "body." That very word
anchors us in the world of reality and guards against the
recurrent religious tendency to "spiritualize" everything
until it becomes vaporized in unreality and self-decep-
tion. In the field of ethics, for example, this error can and
does appear. We can become so involved in philosophical
discussions of what love really is, so entangled in theological disquisitions on love in "mystical" terms, that we stop
doing anything concrete for our neighbor. It was just this
"spiritualizing" in the false sense of the term which provoked St. John to write so bluntly, "But if a man says, 'I
love God,' while hating his brother, he is a liar. If he does
not love the brother whom he has seen, it cannot be that
he loves God whom he has not seen" (I Jn. 4:20).

Perhaps the point can be illuminated by looking at a
great Pauline appeal in Romans 12:1. The New English
Bible translates the verse "Therefore, my brothers, I implore you by God's mercy to offer your very selves to him:
a living sacrifice, dedicated and fit for his acceptance, the
worship offered by mind and heart." The Greek word
Paul uses is "bodies," but the New English Bible translates
"your very selves." Of course this fact neatly supports
what was said above about the biblical meaning of the
word "body." Yet when this verse is echoed in the Book
of Common Prayer, the liturgist writes "we here present
our *selves,* our *souls* and *bodies"* (italics added). To think
of offering ourselves to God is more true to what Jesus
commands, since not every Christian is called to physical
martyrdom. Likewise, someone could get himself mar-
tyred as a Christian simply because he was a masochist or
an exhibitionist, or hoped to force God to save him. Such
a motive would not be self-offering but self-asserting. On

the other hand we can deceive ourselves about how thoroughly we have offered our lives to God and find that the plain words of First John describe us exactly. The truth is shown much more clearly when there is some concrete need to be met, some specific injury to be forgiven, some particular task to be performed, or some real cross to be borne.

Similarly the word "body" makes it clear that we are called to participate in a specific self offered to the Father in a real obedience. We are united to Jesus, not just to some vague ideal. We are saved by him, not by some myth about him. He was "born of the Virgin Mary and crucified under Pontius Pilate"; he lived at a specific time in history; and he lived a specific life. We are summoned to faith in him, not faith in some generalized "Christian spirit" which we can interpret to fit our own preconceptions. To seek his will we must remember that he said certain specific things, performed certain specific actions, and gave certain specific commands. Something of this concern lies behind St. John's insistence that we must "test the spirits, to see whether they are from God" (I Jn. 4:1). St. John's gospel includes the promise that the Spirit will lead us into all the truth. "However, when he comes who is the Spirit of truth, he will guide you into all the truth; for he will not speak on his own authority, but will tell only what he hears; and he will make known to you the things that are coming" (Jn. 16:13). Yet the Holy Spirit will not contradict Jesus; he only helps us penetrate more surely what Jesus has already taught. "Your Advocate, the Holy Spirit whom the Father will send in my name, will teach you everything, and will call to mind all that I have told you" (Jn. 14:26). We are made Christians as he lives in us and we in him. We share in that offered self; we take the bread which is his body.

Do this for the remembrance of me

Once again we need to recall that what a word means to us may not be the same as what it meant when Jesus spoke it and the disciples heard it. "Remembrance" is one of those problem words. For us remembering suggests having a mental image of a past event, an image that may have some psychological effect but is still not real. Is that what it meant to Jesus and to other Jews whose ways of thinking are revealed in Scripture? Biblically it is quite clear that remembering means making present. For example, Jeremiah 31:34 reads, "No longer need they teach one another to know the Lord; all of them, high and low alike, shall know me, says the Lord, for I will forgive their wrongdoing and remember their sin no more." When their sins are forgiven, the trespasses are no longer remembered and no longer exist. Again the bewildered mother of the dying child cries to Elijah, "What have I to do with thee, O thou man of God? art thou come unto me to call my sin to remembrance, and to slay my son?" (I Kg. 17:18, Authorized Version) If her sins are remembered, they are present with all their deadly effect, and so her son is brought to death. We need not discuss here her lamentable theology of retribution; rather we need only notice how "remembering" means "making present."

Added understanding comes from reading Numbers 10:9, "When you go into battle against an invader and you are hard pressed by him, you shall raise a cheer when the trumpets sound, and this will serve as a reminder of you before the Lord your God and you will be delivered from your enemies." When the Lord remembers his loving purpose toward Israel, his saving power is present to rescue them. This biblical thought is especially noteworthy since New Testament scholarship urges us to understand

Jesus' words in such a way that the Father is doing the remembering.[1] When Jesus is thus "remembered," the Kingdom of God being realized in him is present. In our egocentricity we tend to emphasize whether we do or do not remember Jesus. What really matters is that the Father does; only then does our remembering have some place as it opens our lives more widely to the Jesus who is present.

For several centuries Christians fussed terribly about this question. Catholics stressed the Real Presence, while many Protestants would shout "memorial." Then came the happy day when biblical scholarship finally had the sense to ask what "remember" meant in biblical thought. Now we recognize that we cannot separate remembering and being present if we understand what Jesus meant and what the disciples certainly would have believed he was saying. It is of course wonderful that this unfortunate, even though sincerely held, misunderstanding between Christians has been solved. Yet at least as important is the assurance that when we "do this" as Jesus commanded, he is really present. We need him and we want him. We seek him and he seeks us, in prayer, in meditation, and in and through other persons as we love them and they love us. Yet at times our prayers seem made of lead, and our love for others can be so mixed in its motivations and so uncertain in its results. How much it matters, then, to know that here he is present, not because we are good enough, or pray enough, or even remember well enough. He is here because he has promised to be present and because the Father has remembered and made it so.

[1]Joachim Jeremias, *The Eucharistic Words of Jesus,* Oxford: Blackwell, 1955, p. 162 f.

10. After Supper

After supper he took the cup of wine;
and when he had given thanks, he gave
it to them,
and said, "Drink this, all of you:
This is my Blood of the new Covenant,
which is shed for you and for many for
the forgiveness of sins.
Whenever you drink it, do this for the
remembrance of me."

Why does Jesus perform two acts, taking the bread and then taking the cup? Why two words of interpretation, one for the bread and another for the cup? Of course the image of blood certainly spells a sacrifice, but the words "for you" about the bread also spell sacrifice. So one might think that we have here a bit of repetition for the sake of emphasis, akin to Jesus' use of twin parables to give a kind of one-two punch. Although true, this reply is not wholly adequate, for two reasons. First, the words of interpretation are similar but not so close as to constitute mere repetition. Second, it seems that the tendency in the transmitting of Christian tradition was to increase the parallelism so that the two acts become more uniform.[1]

[1]Hans Conzelmann, *First Corinthians,* Philadelphia: Fortress Press, 1975, p. 201; Jeremias, *Eucharistic Words,* p. 110.

Of course the opinions of biblical scholarship are not infallible, but the warnings should make us cautious.

The most frequent explanation, and a reasonable one, is that the bread and the cup, the body and the blood, as separated things foretell a violent death.[2] We can put some confidence in this explanation, since it does not drag in some new idea of our own invention. The words "which is shed for you" very plainly tell of a violent death. Jesus' death was a real death, and it was violent. As we rejoice in the rescue of the Passion, as we laud and hymn the victory of the Resurrection, we may forget the harsh violence and brutality of the death of Jesus. God can and does bring good out of our pain, but that does not change the fact that the pain hurts. It was no different for Jesus. But Christ's death can remind us that sin does matter, that our evil actions do really hurt others and can be fatal to them and to ourselves. In this age we have become increasingly aware that human motivations are very complex, that we often do unintended wrongs because of emotional pressures often unperceived, and that moral decisions are not always simple matters of black or white. We rightly shy away from simplistic judgments, and we suspect that our ancestors sometimes cried "sin" prematurely or unfairly. How easily, however, we may let the pendulum swing too far the other way. There is undoubtedly truth in viewing a war as a kind of psychotic episode in the social organism, but we dare not forget that there are also dead bodies of human beings, lives abruptly ended, and families weeping bitter tears. Evil does kill, and that is true also of the evil we have done. The hasty word that cuts, the selfish indifference that chills, the absorbed self-interest that tramples upon someone else—such things as these do take

[2]Jeremias, *Eucharistic Words*, p. 144.

their toll, and the cost is great. The price is death, and we dare not romanticize that brutal fact.

This is my Blood of the new Covenant

Is there, however, still some particular aspect of the self-offering of Jesus which the cup makes clear? We would expect that there would be some distinction, since the word of interpretation is different from that used with the bread. Discovering that particular meaning is made more difficult by the slight variations in wording found in our two earliest sources. Some scholars prefer St. Mark's account, "This is my blood of the covenant, shed for many" (14:24), as the more primitive and so stress the word "blood." Others give precedence to Paul's account, "In the same way, he took the cup after supper, and said: 'This cup is the new covenant sealed by my blood. Whenever you drink it, do this as a memorial of me'" (I Cor. 11:25), and so emphasize the word "covenant." We cannot wait until that debate is settled, if indeed it ever can be. Fortunately we do not have to wait, because the two images so overlap that the meaning is reasonably clear.

First the word "blood." In the Bible the blood is the life (Gen. 9:4–5, Lev. 17:11). The bread shows Jesus' self-offering; the cup manifests the living aspect of that self-offering, the power of it, the dynamic element of it. A related point is that in Old Testament thought blood is poured out not for the sake of its shedding but for its being made available for use. The stress is not on the dying, which the shedding of blood requires, but on the sprinkling of the blood to cleanse (Heb. 9:19–21). Similarly in Pauline thought the sacrifice of Christ brings to the believer not just forgiveness of the past but a new power for a different quality of life (Rom. 8:1–2, 10). This approach suggests, then, that whatever is different about the meaning of the cup is to be found in the life-giving, cleansing, invigorating power of the offering Jesus presents.

Next, the word "covenant." It matters little whether Jesus did or did not originally use the word "new," because the covenant he establishes is a new one. Every Jew present in that Upper Room knew there was already a covenant established by God; when Jesus grants another one, it is necessarily a new covenant. Old Testament prophecy foretold a new covenant: "But this is the covenant which I will make with Israel after those days, says the Lord; I will set my law within them and write it on their hearts; I will become their God and they shall become my people. No longer need they teach one another to know the Lord; all of them, high and low alike, shall know me, says the Lord, for I will forgive their wrongdoing and remember their sin no more" (Jer. 31:33–34). The newness has to do with the interior quality of the covenant and the immediacy of the relationship between God and the believer. In the New Testament it is particularly the work of the Holy Spirit to give this interior moral guidance and to achieve the divine indwelling. It is the Spirit who gives life, and it is the Spirit who empowers the new kind of living which transcends external rules and codes. The self-offering of Jesus establishes the new covenant and opens the way to the gift of the Spirit.

So the two images of blood and of covenant overlap. Both emphasize the life-giving, power-enabling, cleansing and renewing aspect of Christ's sacrifice. The unity of the two images is reinforced by recalling that in Scripture there is no covenant without the shedding of blood: "Thus we find that the former covenant itself was not inaugurated without blood. . . . Indeed, according to the Law, it might almost be said, everything is cleansed by blood and

without the shedding of blood there is no forgiveness"
(Hebrews 9:18, 22). The meaning of the bread and that of
the cup cannot be sought as isolated elements, because
Jesus broke the bread and took the cup on the same occasion and in the same context. Insofar as there is some
distinction between the two, it seems clear that the cup
especially stresses the life-giving purpose of the sacrifice
of Christ Jesus. We are then to remember not simply his
goodness in dying for us, but also the positive purpose of
his sacrifice of himself. We are to be thankful not only for
forgiveness of the past, but also for the promise of a new
kind of life for the future. By the sprinkling of his blood
we are not only cleansed but also made new, that "he may
live in us and we in him."

Whenever you drink it, do this
for the remembrance of me

"Do this" is a present imperative, meaning "keep on
doing this." Hence the Church down through the centuries has centered her worship in the eucharistic liturgy, in
this distinctively Christian act. The command to repeat
the supper is found in First Corinthians 11:24–25, a letter
written before any of the Gospels were composed in their
present form. Some theologians, however, have doubted
that Jesus commanded the repetition of the rite because
the words "do this" are not found in the Gospel accounts
of the Last Supper. One may reply that Paul's account is
the oldest, but even more than that can be considered.
Recent New Testament study makes it clear that individual stories about Jesus' actions or individual sayings of
Jesus were repeated over and over again until the Gospels
(or their fragmentary ancestors) became fixed in some
written form. We need to ask why some sayings were thus

repeated, while other utterances of Jesus were not. Clearly the early Christians repeated stories or sayings which had immediate significance for the Church, as guides for the life of the community, for moral decisions facing individuals, for teaching purposes, and so forth. Hence the Gospel accounts of the supper were not handed on for the sake of preserving history but as guides for the Church in her worship and her life. In other words, the memory of the Last Supper was preserved to help the community "keep on doing this." The commandment is not repeated in the story; the story is told because the command is being obeyed. As one scholar puts it, the command to repeat "intrinsically . . . is already given with the transmitting as such."[3]

We may then be assured that continuing to "do this" is intended by Jesus. Obeying the Lord is right, whether we do or do not understand fully why he commands as he does. Assuredly, however, his intent is more than the simple external performance of the rite. The "do this" also includes that for which the rite was designed, our sharing in his obedient self-offering and our participating in the power of living in a new way. To "do this" means offering ourselves to the Father's will in union with Jesus' sacrifice, which alone empowers any efforts of our own. At times we may wonder if the external "do this" is all we ever do or will ever be capable of doing. Yet it is an opening of the door to Jesus; it is a prayer that he will take our pathetic little bit of obedience, immerse it in his own full obedience, and thus make real the intent he has for the service rendered by our lives. Fully to "do this" is at least something we must allow him to accomplish in us and through us.

[3]Conzelmann, *First Corinthians,* p. 200, n. 83.

11. Therefore We Proclaim

Therefore we proclaim the mystery of faith:
Christ has died.
Christ is risen.
Christ will come again.
We celebrate the memorial of our redemption, O Father,
in this sacrifice of praise and thanksgiving.
Recalling his death, resurrection, and ascension,
we offer you these gifts.
Sanctify them by your Holy Spirit
to be for your people the Body and Blood of your Son,
the holy food and drink of new and unending life in him.
Sanctify us also
that we may faithfully receive this holy Sacrament,
and serve you in unity, constancy, and peace.

A corporate acclamation in the middle of the Consecration Prayer is for many of us a rather startling thing and for some unwelcome. For many years we have been accustomed to a hushed stillness at this part of the liturgy, and we have found it right and satisfying. Now we are expected to join in a vigorous affirmation of faith, perhaps even singing it. We may have a special need to ask why this affirmation has been recommended and what it means. The liturgical authorities claim that it is desired—some would insist that it is required—to strengthen the *anamnesis* or "remembering" portion of the Consecration Prayer. We have already considered the meaning of the word "remembrance" and have seen that it helps us understand how the one sacrifice of Christ can affect us in this moment. Perhaps, however, we can get at the problem afresh by noticing that there are three time references in this acclamation: the past (Christ has died), the present (Christ is risen), and the future (Christ will come again).

What difference does that past reference make? It reminds us that our salvation was achieved by the Passion of Christ a long time ago. Before we were able to do anything, even before we were born, Christ died and was raised. By his work, and the Father's acceptance of his self-offering, our rescue was achieved. This bluntly tells us that we do not save ourselves, that we cannot earn salvation, and that we do not have to attempt anything so impossible. It puts us in our right place, for we are creatures receiving life from the Creator, and we are captives needing to be rescued by the Savior. So "we celebrate the memorial of our redemption"; we do not concoct our rescue. Likewise we offer the "sacrifice of praise and thanksgiving." We praise Jesus' goodness in saving us, and we are thankful for it. We serve him thankfully because he has loved us; we do not serve grudgingly in order that we might coax him into loving us.

How easily, however, we can forget these familiar truths. How almost irresistibly do we slide back into thinking of the Christian life as a moral code to be obeyed, lest we arouse God's anger, or as a character development course intended to wring a passing grade from a reluctant Divine Examiner. Or else we seek to save God's world for him and then either discover that we have become "benevolent" dictators or else become disillusioned when our attempts to make the world right seem to go awry. One of the things that can help us avoid these perils is the obvious fact that salvation was achieved before we even appeared on the stage of human history. How humbling, but also how great.

Christ is risen

Now the present time reference, indicated by the words "Christ is risen." Because he has been raised, because he reigns in eternity, he can be present to us here and now. This truth we have already considered, but there are other implications of the fact that he is risen. The New Testament more frequently uses the passive voice—he has been raised. This fact reminds us that the Resurrection tells us something about the Father as well as something about Christ. An important element in the Resurrection is its evidence that the Father has accepted the self-offering of the Son. Easter is God's setting his seal of approval on Jesus, on all that Jesus taught and did. It is a divine assertion, "This is my beloved Son; hear him." Hear him, and believe in what he has accomplished. The sacrifice has been made by the Son and accepted by the Father.

Because the sufficient sacrifice has been offered, we now can dare to "offer these gifts" and can pray, "Sanctify us also." Christ Jesus has presented to the Father the offering that mankind wishes but has been unable to make. Therefore we can now do the little things we would otherwise shrink from attempting. We can offer bread and wine, the very ordinary things of life, so God can transform them. We can offer our ordinary lives, in union with the one fully adequate Life, so God can transform us also. One of the truly impressive experiences of our time in history was being allowed to look at the earth as seen from outer space. What a tiny, fragile ball it seemed to be. Yet tiny as it was, where were we in that televised picture? With difficulty one could trace the outline of a continent, but one could not see even the largest city. What then of my street, my house, or me? We are much more tiny than that little ball, and even more fragile. Then who are we to offer anything to the Creator of that vast space in which the little earth spins? How can we dare offer him ordinary lives such as ours, ordinary things such as bread and wine? We may do it, for Christ is risen, the sacrifice of the Son has been accepted.

The fact that Christ is risen also assures us that these little offerings can be transformed. The Resurrection of Christ not only tells us something about the Father; it also teaches something about the Holy Spirit. It asserts that the Spirit is now given in a new and powerful degree. St. John especially stresses that the gift of the Spirit results from the passion of Christ; "Nevertheless I tell you the truth: it is for your good that I am leaving you. If I do not go, your Advocate will not come, whereas if I go, I will send him to you" (Jn. 16:7). The connection between the Passion and the Spirit's outpouring is vividly symbolized by the way St. John describes the piercing of Christ. "But one of the soldiers stabbed his side with a lance, and at once there was a flow of blood and water. This is vouched for by an eyewitness, whose evidence is to be trusted" (Jn. 19:34–35). Jesus offers himself so that his people may be cleansed, and in the upper room Jesus says, "And for their sake I now consecrate myself, that they too may be consecrated by the truth" (Jn. 17:19). It is because Jesus is crucified and raised, because the Spirit is given, that we can pray, "Sanctify them by your Holy Spirit to be for your people the Body and Blood of your Son" and can continue, "Sanctify us also." Jesus is both a man and the new Man, and so he opens unto mankind the way by which the Spirit can enter the human state, can enter into our human world to bless and cleanse and transform.

This truth may help clarify the puzzling words "to be for your people the Body and Blood of your Son." The Spirit existed before Christ became man; he spoke through the prophets, but intermittently and partially. The perfectly obedient man, Jesus, opens the way to the Spirit's coming in fullness. What hinders our openness to the Spirit? Shame and fear keep us closed up, make us draw into a shell as though turtles or huddle in a defensive ball as though hedgehogs. The Passion and Resurrection, however, tell us that we can now be freed from that shame and fear. Easter says, "The shame is gone, for sin is forgiven, and the scarlet has been made as white as snow." Easter also shouts that the power of sin is broken too, so fear can be cast off along with shame. There is no longer the need to hide because of shame or to curl into a ball because of fear. We can dare to let Jesus open us so the Spirit can enter. The gifts are made the body and blood of the Son, but only God's people know them to be such and will allow them to effect their purpose as such. Others will not or cannot receive them as such and close their lives to inhibit the Spirit's coming. Because Christ is risen the Spirit can come fully, so these humble gifts can be transformed. Likewise our ordinary lives, our spasmodic and flickering desires for holiness, our blundering and groping wish to serve him truly—these too can be transformed. He is risen, and the Spirit is come.

Christ will come again

The future time reference also matters much, with its hope for and promise of "new and unending life in him." Unending life may not by itself be an awfully happy prospect. Imagine going on forever exactly as we are now; that prospect can be a fearful thing. Indeed one of our greatest burdens in a time of trouble or of discouragement is the unjustified assumption that this state will go on and on. We ask with dismay, "How long can I take this?" So it is important to notice the word "new" connected with "unending life." We pray that the Spirit may sanctify the gifts to be for his people "the holy food and drink of new and unending life in him." In him we may "faithfully receive" and in him find trust that we may serve better than before. Now our faith is dim and our prayers for sanctification erratic and timid. Yet Christ will come again, finally and completely; his final coming to complete the transformation assures us that his present coming begins the change in us.

Why do we rejoice that Christ came on earth, comes now in the Eucharist, and will come again? Not simply because we have been redeemed and will attain final salvation. We rejoice also because his coming opens up the possibility that we may serve him, beginning in this life and continuing in some unknown fashion in eternity. Our attempts to serve, however, are so marred and so confused. We would like to serve in unity with others, wholly freed from competitiveness and envy, from resentment at praise withheld or greedy clutching at commendation offered, from concern with how other people judge our serving. We would like to serve with constancy instead of mingling bursts of zeal and interludes of sloth, instead of alternating impatience and procrastination. We wish to serve in peace, allowing Christ to take care of the results, and without the anxiety that comes from trying to impress him, or others, with our worth. This peace can begin as we ponder more deeply the truth that Jesus will come again. It is his final coming which alone will fulfill all that is now partial, cleanse all that is now mixed with some degree of selfishness, and make right all that is now slightly askew. The Kingdom of God is already here, but it is also not yet come fully. So it is not surprising that we are in the same mixed state. This truth does not mean that we should be content with less than our best; rather it means that we must do our best with that peacefulness which springs from knowing that Christ alone is holy, that he alone is Lord. The truly right is drawing nearer; for "Christ will come again." The Christ who will come is the same who has died and who is risen. So the power of the future is present to help us begin to serve "in unity, constancy, and peace."

12. And at the Last Day

*And at the last day bring us with all
your saints into the joy of your eternal kingdom.*

"Joy" and "the last day" seem to form a very unlikely combination of ideas. For someone quite familiar with the Bible, the expression "last day" evokes the thought of divine judgment, an association not conducive to dancing in the streets and clapping hands with glee. For others "last day" also suggests the ending of something, and endings often have a sorrowful tinge. The phrase calls up, for example, memories of the last day of our college years, the bittersweet hours of graduation day. Yet perhaps that idea of graduation day may help us perceive the connection of joy with the end of earthly history.

Suppose there were no graduation day? We would never have to leave the ivy-covered halls of alma mater, but that blessing would be a dubious one. Imagine going on and on forever in college, preparing always for some task on which we never begin to work.

For many today life seems to be like that, an affair with no purpose, no goal, no point. In the last century the Western world was bathed in a naive optimism, as men believed the world was steadily improving in an irresistible and irreversible fashion. Such optimism has been given a severe jolting by a number of things. Two world wars have exposed the thin veneer of civilization over the violence of humankind. The Nazi concentration camps appeared in a nation renowned for its educational system and its scientific achievements, and those places of horror reminded men that the beastly and the demonic were more than poetic expressions from ancient mythology. The idea of a gradual enlightenment of mankind appears less certain when we know how much devastation can come from one single idiot playing with an atomic device. If the life of this world be the only one there is, then we may well wonder "Of what value is my life?"

It is just this question which troubles many and banishes joy. Yet the truth of a "last day," the assurance of another stage of life for which this life is a preparation, has much to say about the value of trying to make life better for others today. Even in our own limited experience we have discovered that a number of things make sense on a "last day" which seemed to make no sense at all when they first happened to us. Just so, that ultimate last day will bring an understanding of some of our present burdens that we cannot possess right now. We may find that there was indeed a point to much that today seems pointless, a significant purpose behind much that now appears futile. There is good reason to think of joy in connection with the last day.

With all your saints

The hope of heaven is not a selfish thing, because God is such that eternal life in his presence must involve others. The essence of heaven is being with the Lord, but that Lord is the Creator and Redeemer of mankind. Hence eternal life by its very nature is experienced with all the saints. The corporate nature of salvation is a comfort to us, since we know that selfishness is destructive of others and of ourselves. It is a joyful thing to be assured then that the goodness shown to us will never be at the expense of anyone else and will not be for any other person a cause to feel threatened or cheated. In this world our gladness at an accomplishment or a benefit is sometimes spoiled because someone else does not have it too. Yet in God's kingdom, in the state in which his will is perfectly real-ized, there will be enough goodness for all to be filled. There will be no envy and no need for any; one man's good will never deprive his neighbor, just as no one will find his satisfaction in depriving another. This kind of joy is assured by the truth that it will be life "with all the saints."

There are other joys also in this kind of heaven. One of them will be the gladness of seeing goodness in others, the happiness of perceiving the godliness of the saints. Even on earth we are at times heartened by seeing fine qualities in others; we rejoice at the sight of courage, admire true compassion, and are pleased by any glimpse of genuine holiness. Of course our enjoyment of these qualities here can be stained or twisted because we fear we will look like lesser persons by comparison. In this life we can be upset by the goodness of others, even though we know that such reactions reveal how little goodness there is in us. Yet by the time we are brought to heaven we will have learned humility, and we will be able to enjoy the fact that some-one else is a saint. What a wonderful thing that will be and how great if something of it could be attained before then.

Another source of gladness will be the pleasure of being with the saints. Even here we are excited at the prospect of meeting some truly fine human being. One of the joys of life is meeting someone who has done great things or someone who is great as a person, quite apart from anything he or she may have done. If this be one of the good things of this life, might we not anticipate the same on an even higher level in the next? Some of these saints we hope to be with are ones whose names we know but whom we would like to know much better. Of course each of us will have his own special list. There was an older priest who looked forward to visiting at length with Erasmus, and indeed he may have chosen wisely even if others would not be as enthusiastic about his choice. A former New Testament professor often spoke of his desire to find out from St. Paul whether that certain epistle was written to the North or the South Galatians. This writer believes he has some more urgent questions for St. Paul, as well as a desire to get to know Julian of Norwich, Walter Hilton, and Bishop King of Lincoln. Your list will be different, but it is your own and so it should be.

Then too each of us has a special group of persons who made particular gifts to his or her own self-development —parents, friends, a teacher, a doctor, a priest, or someone else. Probably there are some who meant a lot to us, and we never told them so but now want to very much. Perhaps there are some whose contributions we did not recognize until it was too late to thank them here. There might even be someone who wants to tell us something like that too. We will most likely be surprised by this news and astonished at who is thanking us. There will also be surprises at who the saints will be, but they will be happy surprises. The deepest joy of heaven will be the presence of the Lord, but every trace of goodness is a fragment of his holiness and a product of his action. So we may be assured that he will smile as we find joy "with all the saints."

The joy of your eternal kingdom

In God's eternal kingdom there will be gladness at the rightness of everything. It is much more than the fact that things will be right for us; it is even more than their being right for others too. It is the fundamental rightness of everything that will cause the deepest joy. It is this basic rightness to which Jesus alludes in the Beatitudes. It is this righteousness that will bless those who hunger and thirst for it, that will comfort those who now mourn its absence or its incompleteness. When God's will is perfectly realized and his kingdom has fully come, there will no longer be evil in humanity nor will there be any more of that "cussedness of things" we experience here. The hope of heaven is not just the expectation that things will be right for us; it is much more than such a one-dimensional dream. Rather it is the assurance of something much more sweeping and thoroughgoing, the confidence that at last the entire creation will be made right.

Yet the personal element will be present too, since we will be made right also. We are familiar with the haunting words of Revelation 21:4, "And God shall wipe away all tears from their eyes." What brings tears to the eyes of men? Of course physical pain brings them, and other kinds of pain. They come also from the hurts that others feel. Yet some of the most bitter tears are caused by our own actions. They spring from our hurting of others, from our own self-betrayals, from the evaporating of our good resolutions and our transient efforts at reformation, from our own timidity, irresolution, or just plain laziness. To be set free from all of that clutter would indeed be joyful. It is precisely this hope which the Father seeks to give us and which the Spirit works within us to achieve. To have those tears wiped away is a far more worthy ideal of heaven than we often entertain. God's designs are greater than ours, and his intention for us is more than we can even dream. All will be made right, and even we will be made right.

13. As Our Savior Christ

*As our Savior Christ has
taught us, we now pray
"Our Father"*

That "now" we pray "Our Father" suggests that it is appropriate at this moment to approach God in a fashion that has not been suitable before. We may well wonder how that thought could be a sensible one. Has it not always been appropriate to address the Creator as our Father? The same puzzlement was aroused for many by the words in the Book of Common Prayer service, "And now, as our Savior Christ hath taught us, we are bold to say. . . ." Why is it "bold" to call God "Father"? Is he not our Creator whom we can naturally address as Father at any time and without any boldness being required? The question can be answered from a biblical point of view and also from the viewpoint of personal relationships.

First, the biblical teaching is that the coming of Christ brings into being a wholly new situation. St. John and St. Paul both assert this newness, although they use different images to express it. St. John describes it as a change among men and women from being only creatures to being children: "But to all who did receive him, to those who have yielded him their allegiance, he gave the right to become children of God" (Jn. 1:12). Notice his claim that being God's children is a right God gives to believers, not a right they already possess. By God's mercy we are enabled to become something we were not, namely his children. I do not need to become something I already am. Rabbits and caterpillars are his creatures, but they are not his children; cabbages and poison ivy plants are also his creations, but they are not children. Similarly, the person who is brought to belief is given a very different and quite new standing before God.

The same kind of assertion is expressed by St. Paul as a change from the status of a slave to that of a son. He writes in Galatians 4:5–7:

God sent his own Son, born of a woman, born under the law, to purchase freedom for the subjects of the law, in order that we might attain the status of sons. To prove that you are sons, God has sent into our hearts the Spirit of his Son, crying "Abba! Father!" You are therefore no longer a slave but a son, and if a son, then also by God's own act an heir.

It is the Holy Spirit who alone inspires the man of faith to cry "Abba, Father."

Now that some biblical quotations have been made, the reader may feel bludgeoned into silence, objections muzzled. Yet silence may not really be assent, and some readers may still wonder why John and Paul say what they do. What is so extraordinary about calling God "Father"? In biblical thought sonship involves likeness in character, a conception vividly expressed in our familiar, though non-biblical, expression "a chip off the old block." In chapter 8 of the fourth gospel the opponents of Jesus resent his claim to bring them freedom (from sin) and assert, "We are Abraham's descendants; we have never been in slavery to any man" (Jn. 8:33). In the course of his reply Jesus states, "If you were Abraham's children, you would do as Abraham did. As it is, you are bent on killing me, a man who told you the truth, as I heard it from God. That is not how Abraham acted" (Jn. 8:39b–40). They wish to murder the innocent, and their character is not like that of Abraham. Rather their character is that of the devil, which shows they are his sons. "Your father is the devil and you choose to carry out your father's desires" (Jn. 8:44a). Sonship is demonstrated by the child's likeness to his father.

If I call God my Father, then the implication is that I am like him. Even more serious is the implication that he is somewhat like me. What boldness is required for a human being even to risk such an implication. The "fatherhood of God" is such a familiar phrase that we seldom perceive what incredible assertions are suggested by the words. Jesus is the only Son of God, not only in his being but also in the sense of likeness of character. Only after the Incarnation, only after Jesus unites us to himself by baptism and faith, can we dare to call God "Father." For it is only when Christ lives in us that we can be made like God.

Second, calling God "Father" is a matter of our personal relationship with him. We can call on him as Father only when we can feel and believe that he looks on us in a fatherly way. Yet when did it become possible for men to see the Lord of the Universe in that light? It happened when, and only when, God sent his Son into the world to save us. A brilliant and moving book by Joachim Jeremias has taught us to see how new and surprising it was when Jesus called God "Abba." "Abba" was a very familiar and rather tender word, used by a Jewish boy only in talking to his own father.[1] In no source at all is there any evidence

[1]Joachim Jeremias, *Abba. Studien zur neutestamentlichen Theologie und Zeitgeschichte*, Gottingen, 1966. See also, Jeremias, *New Testament Theology*, New York: Scribner's, 1971, p. 61 ff.

that a Jew dared to use that term in addressing God until Jesus did so. So different was it that it made a powerful impression on the first disciples. Something of the shock of it and the impact of it can still be felt as Paul writes, "To prove that you are sons, God has sent into our hearts the Spirit of his Son, crying 'Abba! Father!' " (Gal. 4:6). Jesus not only prayed that way himself, he taught such as us to pray the same way. In him we mere creatures, and sinful ones besides, can be bold to cry "Abba." Even with his encouragement, indeed even with his command, we could not act that way unless he first had shown us how intensely fatherly the Father really is. "Now" we can see the fatherhood of God, because of the birth, the life, the death, and the resurrection of Jesus Christ. Those events assure us that the Creator is indeed our Father and would have us call on him as such.

Now

Now that Christ has come, we can address God differently. Yet the "now" is used at this particular point in the Communion Service. Is there any significance in that placement? Why now, rather than earlier or later, do we pray "Our Father"? The invitation to pray in this amazing fashion comes right after the Consecration Prayer, and we need to ask why it is given just at this moment. It comes here, not just in the Second Service but in many other liturgies also, for a particular reason. We have seen that remembering means making present. The Christ now present in a special way is the crucified and risen Christ. He is eternal and his self-offering is eternal. He has brought us and our moment in the stream of time into that eternal moment which not only proves the fatherhood of God but in which the Father's will to save is most powerfully acting. So in this "now" we can be bold to cry what at other moments we would tremble to say.

In the Consecration Prayer we have been forcibly reminded that God made us for himself, that when we made ourselves captives he sent his Son to rescue us, "to live and die as one of us." The Spirit has led us to pray that we may be sanctified also, by being united to Christ who alone is holy, in whom alone is true righteousness. Yet during his time on earth, Jesus Christ did not just proclaim salvation; he achieved it. So when present now he not only tells us about his saving work; he effects it too. As he lives in us and we are made to live in him, we now can pray in this new and wonderful way. Now we pray, "Our Father."

Our Father

Since God is our Father, we are his sons and daughters. Yet we may not feel like it, and we may not appear to be such. Others may look at us and question (either silently or quite loudly) our relationship to God. Indeed we may not only share their doubts but be even more certain that our sonship or daughtership is dubious indeed. Just as human beings may imagine that they can live as they please once they have been baptized, others may doubt the reality of their status as children of God even though they have been baptized. We know something of what a Christian ought to be, and we are pained and uneasy because we are still so far from being like that. Others may look at us and doubt that our baptism achieved anything, and we may feel the same way.

The problem cannot be passed off as simply an excess of emotion or as something that happens only to a handful of anxiety-prone misfits. Therefore it is most helpful to read carefully a Johannine passage that deals with the issue.

How great is the love that the Father has shown to us! We were called God's children, and such we are; and the reason why the godless world does not recognize us is that it has not known him. Here and now, dear friends, we are God's children; what we shall be has not yet been disclosed, but we know that when it is disclosed we shall be like him, because we shall see him as he is (I Jn. 3:1–2).

We are God's children, because he has called us such. His word is powerful and accomplishes what he speaks. At creation he said "Light" and there was light. The same creative power today says "Son" or "Daughter," and we are truly made such. If we will then keep the doors open, will allow that creative goodness of God to go on working, then the Spirit within will in time bring forth the fruits of living that are appropriate to the sons and daughters of God. It is not our goodness that makes us God's children. He makes us such, and he achieves whatever goodness eventually appears in us to fit the new standing he has given us.

This matter can be illuminated further by noting Paul's use of adoption as an image to describe what God does in us and for us. Suppose I am invited to live in someone's family, am treated warmly and lovingly as a child of the family. It is a wonderful life, but I am still there more or less on sufferance. What, then, if that family should go on to adopt me? Is anything different? The difference is indeed great. Now I am not just treated as if I were a son; I am a son. The father of the family has made a binding commitment to me, and I have received security. Of course now I have a deeper responsibility to become the kind of child who brings joy to the family and not discredit. The "chip off the old block" should not make others think his father is a disgusting creature. By adopting us in baptism, God brings us into a new status, and he also takes the chance that we may be unruly and unworthy children who disrupt the family's life to an appalling degree. The prodigal son was still a son, and the father loved him as such even when he behaved in such a selfish and discreditable way.

Yet of course there is still unhappiness and anxiety because we are not yet what we ought to be and want to be. Help comes from recalling some words written by one who tried harder perhaps than anyone else to be what a son ought to be. St. Paul wrote,

It is not to be thought that I have already achieved all this. I have not yet reached perfection, but I press on, hoping to take hold of that for which Christ once took hold of me. My friends, I do not reckon myself to have got hold of it yet. All I can say is this: forgetting what is behind me, and reaching out for that which lies ahead, I press towards the goal to win the prize which is God's call to the life above, in Christ Jesus (Phil. 3:12–14).

Two things are significant in this passage. One is the ongoing aspect of the Christian life. Even Paul must recognize the "not yet" aspect of his growth; it is therefore not surprising that we must do so too. The second truth is even more important, his "hoping to take hold of that for which Christ once took hold of me." What counts is not that we reached out to God but that God reached out to us. It is he who started this business, and he can finish it. When he has completed his work in us, then "we shall be like him because we shall see him as he is" (I Jn. 3:2). We want to be his sons and daughters in our living and not just in official standing. Yet we mere mortals cannot understand him well enough to know what one of his sons or daughters really ought to be. But he does know, and we can let him bring it to pass in his own way and in his own time. Only very dimly can we comprehend what it would be to be made like Jesus. God does know, however, and he bids us pray "Our Father."

14. Eternal God

Eternal God, heavenly Father,
you have graciously accepted us as living members
of your Son our Savior Jesus Christ,
and you have fed us with spiritual food
in the Sacrament of his Body and Blood.

We do not realize how much it means to be accepted until we are thrust into a position in which we are not sure that we are accepted. Let us seek to share the feelings of the young ensign assigned to his first shipboard post as he enters the wardroom for the first time. He may seek a quiet obscurity or he may attempt to create a first impression of sparkling brilliance, but with either approach there is so much uneasy tension and even some artificiality. Or consider the new family in town desiring to find a place in the life of the parish and the community. Family members may be over-eager volunteers for any kind of task in order to gain some recognition and to prove the family's worth, or they may timidly hang around the periphery of the parish's social circle, hoping someone will invite them in. Contrast such feelings with those of the family that is accepted and knows it is welcome. It is just this difference that God desires us to experience in his Church and in his world. He has accepted us, and he wants us to live as accepted persons.

We are not required to deal with the Father as though we were constantly on trial. We do not have to prove ourselves to him; he already knows all about us. We do not need to impress him with our diligence or our creativity, for he is the source of both. Hence we can serve him in a very different spirit, seeking to live as Christians not in order that he may love us but rather because he already loves us. Of course there is demand as well as promise in the teaching of Jesus, but it is the demand of someone who believes in our worth and truly cares about us, someone we want to please and whose opinion of us we seek to justify. There is Someone who believes we are worth the cost of redemption, who cares enough to save us, and has a vision of all that we can become. We seek to grow, therefore, not to placate an angry and suspicious judge, but to have the loving Father rejoice in what we achieve with the life he has given us.

In addition, the truth that he has accepted us means that we can accept ourselves. Of course this fact does not justify a static and complacent inertia. Nothing stands still in this life, and we are constantly moving ahead or drifting backward. Yet we can accept our present selves as the material with which we must and can work. We cannot wait until we become finer persons whom God might approve; we must begin with ourselves as we are, the selves he already loves. To accept oneself is to admit that this is who I am, nothing more but also nothing less. This self is the only one I have to present to God, but he is willing to start right here. Together we can create fuller selves, but we can begin with the present ones because he has accepted us.

As living members of your Son
our Savior Jesus Christ

We may still be uneasy, however, about how God can accept us. Is he not pure light, in whom there is no darkness and to whom darkness is a terrible offense? Can he really overlook the secret things of which we are ashamed? Help comes from remembering the words of a much-loved hymn:

> Look, Father, look on his anointed face,
> And only look on us as found in him . . .
> For lo! between our sins and their reward,
> We set the passion of thy Son our Lord.[1]

We are in Jesus, and Jesus lives in us. So the Father sees us not alone, shivering in our weakness and discouraged by our sinfulness; rather he sees us as members of his Son. That oneness with Christ is not some kind of charade, some pretense in which the Father indulges in order to avoid seeing and condemning our sins. Rather the indwelling of Christ means that we are not hopeless and helpless, we are not doomed forever to keep on repeating all the failures of the past. We are truly worth something because Christ has chosen to dwell in us, to pray and serve and grow in us. God is not playing games and indulging in some merciful bit of artificiality. He sees us in Christ, because we really are in him.

Another noteworthy truth is set forth by those words "members of your Son," namely the fact that there is something for each of us to do, some contribution each of

[1] *The Hymnal,* New York: Church Pension Fund, 1940, 189.

us can make. There are no waste parts in a body; there is a function for every cell. Since we are members of Christ's body, there is some task for us to perform. We may seem unimportant to others, and we may ourselves believe that they are right. We may feel that our life is insignificant, that our talents are very ordinary, and that the world would get along perfectly well if we just disappeared. Yet that is not true. Simply because we are members of the Body of Christ, we know there is something for us to contribute. The arm of the quarterback may get the headlines, but the newspapers remind us that the state of his knees is of great importance too. The doctors would have us remember that the quarterback's effectiveness also depends upon such hidden parts as the spleen and the liver and the adrenal glands. The Body of Christ likewise has many parts; the strength or weakness of each cell affects the power of the whole. A different but effective image is used by a modern poet, who writes:

> In a fabulous
> necklace
> I had to admire
> the anonymous string
> by which the whole thing
> was strung together.[2]

Diamonds and rubies get all the attention, but a strong piece of string is mighty important.

[2]Helder Camara, *The Desert Is Futile,* London: Sheed & Ward, 1971, p. 50.

And you have fed us with
spiritual food

The world looks different after a good dinner. You come home tired, worn out, nagged by a cloud of anxious thoughts. After dinner, however, things do not look so bad, and you find yourself not just plagued by problems but ready to handle a few of them. Of course it is not just that the world looks different; indeed the world *is* different because you are changed. You are changed because you have been fed and your strength has been renewed. A meal does make a difference.

Perhaps this truth may lead us to ask a question. Why should a meal be such a central part of the religious life? Why was a meal so often a vehicle for religious practice in many faiths inside and outside Palestine? What is proclaimed by a meal as a meal, that the instinct of the human race has given it such prominence in religious activity?

A meal bluntly reminds me that I am not self-sufficient; I am dependent upon something outside myself. It is ironic to ponder the space flights of the astronauts. Surely those adventures are a signal demonstration of human brilliance and skill, an awesome display of what man can accomplish. However, how much space, extra weight, and hence added thrust were required because men cannot live without food and water and air? As that space ship soared on its way to the moon, human dependence was revealed every time an astronaut took a bite of food, sipped a little water, or breathed in a little oxygen. How humbling such a realization is, especially in the course of such a magnificent accomplishment.

We do not like to be dependent; we resent the fact and do our best to conceal it. At the center of our religious practice there is the Eucharist, a meal, which among other things says we are dependent. Truth is humbling, but it is also liberating. How does this truth set us free? It frees us from the need to be all-knowing and all-powerful. What a horrible burden is the feeling that everything depends solely upon our own decisions and our own efforts. If we are alone in the world, then we cannot afford to make a single mistake. Every decision must be right and completely right; we must be infallible. Yet there is the nagging awareness that we are not infallible, the worrying fear that we cannot foresee everything and cannot control everything. In reality we sometimes do try to live this way, as if we were all alone in the world and had to hold up the universe all by ourselves. No wonder that we get tired, that we are anxious, that we are afraid to sleep lest the world go astray while our eyes are closed. Then what a relief to be reminded by this Meal that we do not have to be infallible and that we are not alone. We are indeed dependent, and it is all right to admit that God is the Lord and we are creatures. We are in his hands, and there is truly no better place to be. We can be saved from our honest mistakes as well as from those dishonest ones called sins. A meal says I am dependent; this Meal tells me that I must be a responsible adult but do not have to be a little god. Someone else is taking care of that task, and we can trust him to do it well.

In the Sacrament of his Body and Blood

Many of us once learned the catechism, but not all of us. Even those exposed to such instruction are unsure of our memories. So we might ask again what we mean by the term "sacrament." "I mean an outward and visible sign of an inward and spiritual grace given unto us; ordained by Christ himself, as a means whereby we receive the same, and a pledge to assure us thereof" (Book of Common Prayer, p. 581). If we recall any part of those long-ago lessons on the catechism, we most likely remember the "outward and visible sign of an inward and spiritual grace" part of it. We are less likely to recall the words, "ordained by Christ himself," and yet that part of the definition matters greatly. It is because he commanded the Eucharist that we can approach it with confidence. How absurd, how even blasphemous, for us to concoct a service that will make the Son of God visit us. Hence it is so important to know that we did not invent the Supper of the Lord; rather Jesus did. Neither do we make him come; he comes because he has promised to do so.

Because he has ordained this sacrament, we are assured that we are concerned not simply with a symbol but with an effective sign. The sacrament is "a means whereby we receive" the promised grace, because he has ordained it. Once God said, "Let there be light" and light appeared. So now when he says "This is my Body," it happens as the word commands. It is because he has instituted this way of meeting us that the sacrament is also "a pledge to assure us thereof." Our meeting him, or better his meeting us, is something on which we can count. In the upper room Jesus promised, "I will not leave you bereft; I am coming back to you" (Jn. 14:18). This promise he will keep fully at the end of time, but he begins to achieve it now. He comes to be with us and to make his abode in us. So too he will go with us as we leave the altar, go with us into our homes, to our work, to our service in his name. We can have confidence, because Christ's presence depends upon his will and not upon our spasmodic striving. He achieves it, and he pledges it.

15. Send Us Now

*Send us now into the
world in peace.*

Every formulation of the Eucharistic rite reflects the age
in which it is written. This liturgy certainly has its characteristic notes also, and one element is its recurring emphasis on peace and joy. Peace has been a great concern of
this generation, which has desperately longed for solu-
tions to the strife among nations, between races, between
classes of society, and between and within individuals. A
related theme has been the need for joy in human lives
and the recognition that joy is not terribly manifest in the
faces of Christian folk. In the Postcommunion Prayer and
in the Dismissal Responses the words pile up—"peace and
courage," "gladness," "rejoicing in the power of the
Spirit," and so on. The revisers seem determined that we
shall be joyful. Of course this determination is good New
Testament theology. Paul writes, "Be always joyful . . . for
this is what God in Christ wills for you" (I Th. 5:16, 18).
And elsewhere, "For the kingdom of God is not eating
and drinking, but justice, peace, and joy, inspired by the
Holy Spirit" (Rom. 14:17). We are justly reminded that
every Sunday is a little Easter, that every Eucharist pro-
claims Christ not only crucified but also raised. The rejoicing motif is right and true; peace and joy should be manifest among Christians.

So the new service almost invites us to go dancing down the aisle and out into the street, singing and clapping and skipping on our happy way. Yet often we do not feel that way, no matter how theologically proper it would be. What shall we do? Shall we then accept another layer of guilt on top of all we have already? Guilt then makes us more sad, brings more sense of failure, evokes more depression because we are not jubilant. If the result is such, there must be something wrong. Perhaps we need to take another look at this business of peace and joy. Of course we recognize that feeling joyful and at peace is not within our control. Emotions are not subject to the will and therefore do not constitute guilt. Yet even more needs to be said.

Was Jesus always joyful? Clearly there are occasions when he was not dancing gladly. He wept over Jerusalem, and he was distressed by the unbelief shown by those gathered at the tomb of Lazarus. In Gethsemane Jesus experienced bitter agony, and he did not rejoice as the shadow of the cross drew ever nearer. There can be such times in our lives too, and surely there is no need at such periods to pile on some unnecessary guilt and make the gloom thicker still. Jesus was not always joyful, and yet he speaks of peace. Let us then examine more closely this peace of which he speaks.

To his disciples Jesus said, "Peace is my parting gift to you, my own peace, such as the world cannot give. Set your troubled hearts at rest, and banish your fears" (Jn. 14:27). Notice it is "my own peace," or even more literally one could translate "peace, the peace that is mine." What kind of peace was his that he gives to us? Clearly it was not the kind of peace that comes from ease and an absence of trouble. Rather it was a peace that persists in the midst of turmoil. We read in John 12:27, "Now my soul is in turmoil, and what am I to say? Father, save me from this hour. No, it was for this that I came to this hour." He is in turmoil, but this fact does not turn him aside from the path assigned him. His peace, then, is one which springs from trust in the Father and which promotes obedience to the Father's will. It is a peace that springs from knowing that the Father's presence can be counted on, even when the evidence for his presence is pitifully small. Jesus declared, "He who sent me is present with me, and has not left me alone; for I always do what is acceptable to him" (Jn. 8:29). It is that kind of peace that is promised us, and for which we pray as we are sent into the world.

We are helped to have this kind of peace by recalling that Jesus never promised an absence of trouble; on the contrary, he told the disciples that they would have difficulties.

Jesus answered, "Do you now believe? Look, the hour is coming, has indeed already come, when you are all to be scattered, each to his home, leaving me alone. Yet I am not alone, because the Father is with me. I have told you all this so that in me you may find peace. In the world you will have trouble. But courage! The victory is mine; I have conquered the world." (Jn. 16:31–33)

Perhaps it may not seem to matter much that Jesus predicted burdens for his followers, but indeed it does make a difference. We are rightly told by Scripture, by the Church, and by the preachers that God cares about his children and will keep them in his care. This part of the message is true, and it is right that it is proclaimed. Yet we may all too easily imagine that it is the whole of the message and conclude that we have been promised an absence of pain if we will just act as good Christians do. Then when trouble comes we feel cheated and betrayed. How much we need to know that Jesus never promised freedom from trouble. What he did promise is that something can be done with the trouble. After warning, "In the world you will have trouble" (Jn. 16:33), Jesus intercedes, "I pray thee, not to take them out of the world, but to keep them from the evil one" (Jn. 17:15). So the first truth is that Jesus does not promise an easy kind of peace, and we should not feel cheated if we are not given it.

Yet the second truth is even more vital, namely that God can do something with the trouble. The pain, whatever it may be, is not senseless and useless. The peace of which Jesus speaks is the kind that springs from being assured that God is at work to bring good out of evil. Jesus did not rejoice at the prospect of crucifixion, but he said, "And I shall draw all men to myself, when I am lifted up from the earth" (Jn. 12:32). With his fate before his eyes he declared, "In truth, in very truth I tell you, a grain of wheat remains a solitary grain unless it falls into the ground and dies; but if it dies, it bears a rich harvest" (Jn. 12:24). We are assured that God does something creative with our troubles too. Paul's life was anything but serene, and yet he writes, "In everything, as we know, he cooperates for good with those who love God and are called according to his purpose" (Rom. 8:28). Somehow God will bring good out of this painful thing, even though we may not be able to see how he can do it. Occasionally we may glimpse, some time after the event, how he has done it and may perceive what the good result was. But this happens later and not at the time of pain. Indeed in many instances we may never in this life be able to see the good; we may have to wait until eternity makes all things clear. Yet what a difference it makes to have this assurance that no painful event is useless if we let God work on it, that something creative can be wrought from even the most unlikely material. From this conviction there comes a peace that persists in the midst of turmoil. It is not the kind of peace that leads to jubilant skipping and clapping, but it is the kind that keeps us moving ahead in stormy times. Of such a sort was Jesus' peace as he "set his face resolutely towards Jerusalem" (Lk. 9:51).

The peace that fits with the word "resolute" is unlikely to manifest itself in dancing in the streets, but it is consonant with a quiet and lasting kind of joy. It is an inner peace that can persist even in a time of outside turmoil. St. Teresa writes in the *Interior Castle*, "Can any evil be greater than the evil which we find in our own house? What hope can we have of being able to rest in other people's homes if we cannot rest in our own?"[1]

We all know that peace at home helps immeasurably in carrying heavy burdens in our work and our community life. The same is true with another sort of "peace at home," an inner peace coming from confidence in the Lord's love and power. This inner peace is closer to what Jesus had and what he sought for us. "Peace is my parting gift to you, my own peace, such as the world cannot give. Set your troubled hearts at rest, and banish your fears" (Jn. 14:27). We are sent into the world, as Jesus was. In the world we may well find trouble, but the strength God grants is to be used in the world and for it. Since this task is one he assigns, we can approach it with an inner peace, a "peace at home," which has been promised us.

[1]E. Allison Peers, ed., *The Collected Works of St. Teresa*, Vol. II (New York: Sheed and Ward, 1972), p. 217.

16. To Love and Serve You

To love and serve you
with gladness and singleness of heart.

"To love and serve" is a provocative combination of words and also a very proper one. Loving and serving are intimately connected. In many an American home has been heard the exclamation, "If you love me so much, why don't you ever take out the garbage?" Not wholly unrelated is the biblical verse, "If you love me you will obey my commands" (Jn. 14:15). Similarly the requirement to love our neighbors refers to a basic attitude toward others, but the attitude is suspect unless some concrete expression appears. "Suppose a brother or sister is in rags with not enough food for the day, and one of you says, 'Good luck to you, keep yourselves warm, and have plenty to eat,' but does nothing to supply their bodily needs, what is the good of that? So with faith; if it does not lead to action, it is in itself a lifeless thing" (Jas. 2:16–17). Love for God likewise demands serving him, but we need also to remember that he seeks us and not just our service. He wants us to be united to himself, and from this truth comes the rightness of prayer, meditation, and worship. "To love and serve" is a wonderful combination; each requires the other, and either part becomes distorted when attempted by itself.

We go forth to serve God, but how shall we serve? It is so very human to dream of some great action, of something important, perhaps even of something dramatic. After some significant religious experience, no matter what its form may be, we want to do something for God, hopefully something equally as great as our thankfulness to him. Once in a while some individual is called to a significant action and given the opportunity to do an important work. Yet far more frequently nothing like that appears. Instead we go back to the same old job, the same family, the same priest, the same community, the same everything. It seems such a letdown, when God has touched us and made our hearts yearn to serve. We so easily feel that Christianity means doing extraordinary things, and it is humbling to be told that much more often it means doing ordinary things in an extraordinary way. Though we return to the same old duties in the same old place, we can begin to perform them in a new and different fashion. We do the same things, but in a different spirit, with a new degree of patience, a new dedication, a new sense of humor about ourselves, and a strangely different estimate of what is owed to us. Even more remarkable, we might even stop worrying at all about what is due to us and instead rejoice that we have not received what we deserved. In the Gospels we read about a man whom Jesus cured. And then, "The man from whom the devils had gone out begged leave to go with him; but Jesus sent him away: 'Go back home,' he said, 'and tell them everything that God has done for you' " (Lk. 8:38–39a).

With gladness and singleness
of heart

Once again we discover a provocative combination of terms. Gladness is an attractive quality, and singleness of heart is assuredly a great virtue; yet virtue and gladness do not easily fit together in our minds. Singleness of heart is not only something we ought to desire; it is also something that would make any Christian truly glad. How wonderful it would be to live with singleness of heart, with true simplicity of motive. The common lot of humankind is ambivalence, or even worse. We want more than one thing at a time. We want to serve God, but we also want to rest, to be praised by other people, to avoid criticism, to polish our egos and to be at the same time respected for our humility. This is like trying to drive speedily uphill with the brake on. We do not go very fast, and we get terribly tired. We are so inconsistent and so inconstant, simply because we seek more than one thing. Of such a person St. James declares, "He is double-minded, and never can keep a steady course" (Jas. 1:8). Our experience supports this dictum, and we admit that we grow tired because our course is not a straight line but a series of zigzags as we swerve from one desire to another and never reach either goal. The New Testament message, however, is not just a tale of "You ought"; rather it is a promise of "You can." We can be made pure in heart, and God can give simplicity of desire. To be granted such "singleness of heart" will certainly mean "gladness" too.

How does it happen, though, this singleness of heart? In rare instances the change is sudden, a definite turning around of a human life by the power of God. For most, however, the process seems a more gradual affair, a steady but quiet stripping of motives. How does God do it? As an example, let us take a hypothetical priest. He goes off to seminary with what he believes are rather pure motives. He wishes to preach the word of God, to use his sermons to lighten human lives by helping people open up to God's love and God's wisdom. He wants to preach well, because the message deserves his best and because people deserve his best. He does well, and he is praised for it. How sweet is that praise, and perhaps only then does he realize that the desire for it was a hidden piece of the motivation that led him to ordination. Then what shall he do? Of course he can ask to be deposed, but that could ignore the truth that God can use even mixed motives to get us in the right place. So our imaginary priest does not seek escape, and then the stripping begins. In a short while his people come to take for granted that his sermons will be worthwhile. So the praise stops coming; the sermon draws comment only when it is "not up to your usual standard of excellence." Sunday after Sunday stretches before him; the sermons must be done well, because he must speak in God's name to human beings God loves. Enough years of that experience will strip away anyone's motives, and someday the priest discovers a singleness of heart beginning within him.

The same thing occurs in other occupations. Whether preparing tasty dinners, teaching classes well, typing letters neatly and swiftly, or running a lathe with an expert touch, our skill comes to be taken for granted and stripping of motives occurs. Indeed the same thing happens with prayer. It is joyful and thrilling, and hence there is the danger that we may pray because it is so satisfying and not because there are deeper reasons for prayer. Then one is left for a while to keep on praying when no thrill comes, when there is no satisfaction at all, when it seems a hopeless or even deluded business. In such a painful way, the saints tell us, we are brought to a level of prayer that surpasses whatever we imagined before. Whether suddenly or in this more gradual way, God creates singleness of heart, and with it comes gladness too.

17. Let Us Go Forth

Let us go forth into the world,
rejoicing in the power of the Spirit.

In the new liturgy the blessing is optional, and we may wonder why that change was made. The scholars justly remind us that it was apparently a later addition to the Eucharist. Even more important than this historical fact is a theological truth. After receiving the Body and Blood of Christ anything else is by comparison relatively trivial and unimportant. Having been granted this contact with the risen Christ, is it not rather anticlimactic to be given a blessing transmitted by a human agent? These arguments are powerful ones, and we cannot justly accuse the revisers of simply making changes for novelty's sake. Yet can anything be said for the clergyman who continues the former practice? Even though the apologetic does not overthrow the cogency of the scholars' reasoning, can there be any values in the priestly blessing?

As will be noted later, we go forth to serve the Lord, and the momentous truth is that Christ goes with us. We live as Christians with the assurance of his presence in all the events of our earthly days. Yet along the road we also need human caring. God's love comes to us directly, but he also gives it through his other children. By his gift we do have fathers and mothers, brothers and sisters in

Christ, by whose aid we are helped to recognize God's presence and through whom his love can touch us. In the Eucharist Christ gives us himself, but he can also bless us through his people.

An ordained agent who gives an added blessing can also remind us that God can truly work through us too. To the apostles Jesus said, "To receive you is to receive me, and to receive me is to receive the One who sent me" (Mt. 10:40). So we may see more clearly that he does indeed seek to act through us. If he blesses through that bishop or that priest, it is clearly not impossible for him to use me too. We need to know that he does indeed live in us, pray through us, give his love to others through us. When we come to see ourselves more honestly, we may wonder whether we have anything to give to others. We may wonder too how we can presume to speak to others about the Christ, or how we can dare to say what is God's will in the affairs of others. To know that God does bless us through human agents may lead us to greater assurance that he can touch others even through us.

Let us go forth

In the Dismissals we find a common motif, with the injunctions, "Go in peace," and "Let us go forth." The revisers seem determined, and justly so, to get us out of the church and into the world God loves. We must go forth, but we cannot help wondering "Where?" Where will God take me, through what valleys will he lead me, in what experiences of this day will I seek to find his will? It is disquieting to ask such questions, even though we know they are wholly realistic ones. More than a few human beings have found themselves living far away from their childhood scenes and spending their lives in an occupation of which they and their parents never even dreamed. Even if one's whole life story is written in the same place and devoted to anticipated activities, still there are experiences he or she never expected, never dreamed of, never even feared in prospect.

It helps, therefore, to discover that the theme of "going forth" is a frequent one in Scripture. A good-sized portion of the Old Testament deals with Israel's being led out of Egypt and then wandering for a long time along a very circuitous route to the Promised Land. The father of the faithful, Abraham, is especially cited as one who likewise went forth and knew not where. "By faith Abraham obeyed the call to go out to a land destined for himself and his heirs, and left home without knowing where he was to go" (Heb. 11:8). Jesus came out of Nazareth to be baptized by John, and the reality of his human nature forbids our assuming that he knew then every step of the path on which he was entering. St. John rather clearly states that the hour of the Passion was in the Father's hands and unknown to the Son. The same would appear to be true of the road that led to the Passion. Jesus must have shared with us the uncertainty of not knowing where he would walk as he went forth.

From this fact we may learn two truths about our own venture of going out. First, we do not go alone. Jesus said, "As thou hast sent me into the world, I have sent them into the world" (Jn. 17:18). The requirement to "go forth" comes not from scholars who write new liturgies; it comes from Jesus Christ. Yet as he sends us out, he promises also to be with us in our going. In the same high priestly prayer that speaks of our sending, we find him declaring, "I made thy name known to them, and will make it known, so that the love thou hadst for me may be in them, and I may be in them" (Jn. 17:26). We may tremble as we go forth, but we do not walk alone.

Second, we do not go forth for random wandering, we are moving toward a goal. Along the road there are other persons to be loved, and there is service which God desires. The path may have many strange twists and some very peculiar turns, but it is going somewhere. The Jesus who sends us forth has also told us of the goal he intends: "Father, I desire that these men, who are thy gift to me, may be with me where I am, so that they may look upon my glory, which thou hast given me because thou didst love me before the world began" (Jn. 17:24). The liturgy writers may seem more anxious for us to "go forth" than we are; indeed we may cynically wonder if they are as eager to go out themselves as they are to urge us forth. Yet what really matters is what God desires. The Spirit led the author of the Epistle to the Hebrews to exclaim,

And what of ourselves? With all these witnesses to faith around us like a cloud, we must throw off every encumbrance, every sin to which we cling, and run with resolution the race for which we are entered, our eyes fixed on Jesus, on whom faith depends from start to finish: Jesus who, for the sake of the joy that lay ahead of him, endured the cross, making light of its disgrace, and has taken his seat at the right hand of the throne of God. (Hebrews 12:1–2)

Who is it who sends us out? It is Jesus who walks the road with us and awaits us at the goal. It is Jesus, the Son of that Father who in his infinite love made us for himself.